WEAVING AN OTHERWISE

WEAVING AN OTHERWISE

In-Relations Methodological Practice

Edited by Amanda R. Tachine and
Z Nicolazzo

Foreword by Leigh Patel

Afterword by K. Wayne Yang

Routledge
Taylor & Francis Group

NEW YORK AND LONDON

First published 2022 by Stylus Publishing, LLC.

First Edition, 2022

Published 2023 by Routledge
605 Third Avenue, New York, NY 10017
4 Park Square, Milton Park, Abingdon, Oxon OX14 4RN

*Routledge is an imprint of the Taylor & Francis Group,
an informa business*

Library of Congress Cataloging-in-Publication Data

Names: Tachine, Amanda, editor. | Nicolazzo, Z., editor. | Patel, Leigh, writer
    of foreword. | Yang, K. Wayne, writer of afterword.
Title: Weaving an otherwise : in relations methodological practice / edited by
    Amanda Tachine and Z Nicolazzo ; foreword by Leigh Patel ; afterword by
    K. Wayne Yang.
Description: First edition. | Sterling, Virginia : Stylus, 2022. | Includes
    bibliographical references and index.
Identifiers: LCCN 2022015442 |
    ISBN 9781642673326 (cloth) | ISBN 9781642673333 (paperback)
Subjects: LCSH: Qualitative research--Methodology. | Qualitative research-
    -Moral and ethical aspects. | Qualitative research--Social aspects. |
    Decolonization.
Classification: LCC H62 .W3797 2022 | DDC
    001.4/2--dc23/eng/20220607
LC record available at https://lccn.loc.gov/2022015442

ISBN 13: 978-1-64267-332-6 (hbk)
ISBN 13: 978-1-64267-333-3 (pbk)
ISBN 13: 978-1-00-344864-8 (ebk)

DOI: 10.4324/9781003448648

In gratitude to the weavers from generations back who dreamed textiles of the future, that is now our present.

—Amanda

To Freeses Pond; I hope the views, smells, and sounds from the banks are beautiful, Mom.

—Z

CONTENTS

PART THREE: AFTER

FOREWORD

Forward, or Rather, Toward

In *Weaving an Otherwise: In-Relations Methodological Practice*, the weavers, Amanda R. Tachine and Z Nicolazzo, dreamt into reality this collection of moving chapters with writers, thinkers, and cultural workers. These chapters provide us stories, tools, and ideas to release. We might not have known, with our minds, that we needed release, but likely our bodies knew. As Cynthia Dillard, Nana Mansa II of Mspeasam, Ghana, and deeply respected and beloved educator in relation to many traditions, most deeply Black women educators, has long taught us, we've often been made to equate chef-proof "recipes" and logarithms that reinforce the coloniality logics that can only be anointed by seemingly objective truth. Cynthia Dillard's resounding work invites to both release and to remember what we've been taught to forget, in part, that ways of knowing are not a collection of ideas but sets of practices and relations. For too long, researchers have sought to know, and those researched have been sought, even seduced into a tacit agreement of transaction and extraction.

We have needed this book for a long time. It is not coincidental that the words, the thoughts, the very personhoods partially etched in these pages have answered a call of weaving, relationality, practice, and otherwise. Weaving is a long-standing practice of cultural survivance. The cover of this beautiful book features the textile artistry created by Amanda as an act of relation, love, and ceremony. That the picture of this work of art that provides warmth graces the cover of this book is testimony to the fact that Native women's existence is an act of survivance. Gerald Vizenor's precise use of survivance is neither survival nor resistance, as one of the chapters, coauthored by two deeply gifted Native women, reminds us. Weaving is a way of repeating a pattern to serve the material function of warmth and the symbolic soul work of being grounded in relation. Quilts, woven by women from many different places and times, have strikingly familiar patterns, a reminder to us of the power and call for rematriation that is also present in so many of the chapters here.

As several authors note, these chapters were written in the COVID-19 pandemic, an airborne virus that mutates as it is passed from one being to another. If there is one lesson that we should learn from this global pandemic, which is so beautifully woven in these chapters, it is that we are all connected. The question that this volume so beautifully addresses is "How then can we be with ourselves and others out of duty, responsibility, and calling to be in right relation?" That this volume came into existence in a global pandemic and its intertwined global grief is a testimony to the collective and a prayer for who and what we've lost. Related to the words that Sandy Grande and Teresa McCarty wrote in their introduction to a 2018 themed journal issue addressing "Indigenous elsewhere," crafted during the mass Native and coconspirators' protection of water at Standing Rock, "Within the context of the academy, such pulls [of familial caregiving] are often made to feel like a pulling *away* rather than *toward*. . . . During this time, writing seemed like both a necessity and a distraction. We were, along with the rest of the world, compelled by the historic gathering." These words hold renewed and a specifically different gravity for a volume that was crafted into being while all these cultural workers were encountering themselves in grief, in longing, in fear, and in reverence of connection. Connection and relation is what allows for the encountering of ourselves and otherwise, woven within and across time and space. This volume invites us to break up with and release what so many of our bodies, whether in graduate school or under mythologies of what it "takes" to get tenure, have been trying to tell us: Don't fall for the hustle.

The many textbooks of how to do research all perpetuate the same falsehood: that there is a playbook, a field guide, a chronology, a technology for conducting research. Theory is a constant presence, echoed in the words of children asking "Why?" who are then quickly labeled troublemakers, as Carla Shalaby teaches us. Theory is always present but somehow, methods are catalogued, categorized, and hold imaginary borders between this method and that method, and perhaps even more ludicrously, that methods are separate from theory. What a lie, and my goddess that lie has enjoyed a long life. This collection offers a reprieve, in fact, a hospice, a kind escort to dying because it is time. We are invited to a solidity in unsettling the colonial magician's tools of distracting narratives that methods have been void of person or context. Here, we are offered no how-to's, but thoughtful ways that tell us, through stories and context, reflections on how these thinkers have made their way to be in relation to knowledge, each other, those who have come before, and those yet to come. All of which makes this collection both precise in contexts of time and space and quite likely relevant for many generations.

It has been over 20 years since Professor Linda Tuhiwai Smith offered these straightforward words, that to Indigenous peoples "research" is a dirty word. In this volume, we are offered not a facile reclamation of that term but a contextualized tussling with the hard, violent histories of research and the intersections that universities and museums have, as well as the always available ways to be otherwise, to dream, to imagine and create freedom through knowledge and relation. As StrikeMoMa's second platform states so clearly, "Their archives are our receipts." This book is full of not just receipts but openings, groundings, and points of view for the always necessary jump-off.

As I read the ways that these human beings, the thinking partnerships and collaboratives, describe their relationship to knowledge, including the need to create necessary, perhaps impermanent boundaries, I found myself returning to the echo, the pattern, the arc of a single word: *generative.*

To be in right relation with dynamics of power, history, and futurities we need to be generative—not producing for production's sake, but generative as a form of capaciousness, as offering, as responsibility that does not seek to overdetermine the future and also recognizes responsibility as duty. That spaciousness is anything but naïve. On the contrary, it is from a view of the centuries-long rule that colonial logics have had over the academy, as well as a regard and engagement in the always constant decolonial presence in the colonial, as Ngugi wa Thiong'o has taught us for decades. That space of decolonial in the colonial is where capaciousness is encounter, resized over and over again as our resistance and creations take temporary formation. And that spaciousness will make mistakes. One of the bravest moves this volume makes is to acknowledge the obvious: In striving for knowledge practices that create liberation while tearing down hierarchy, we will make mistakes. The mistakes are where we practice; we unlearn to make room for new learning. Any artist or athlete knows it is in practicing again and again that allows for difference to become apparent. And when we are not practicing, we are not practicing that chance to apprehend, encounter, and learn from difference. Because education has for so long allowed itself to be overdetermined by its rather low rank in universities, it has too often refused to learn from mistakes, in favor of rushing from one innovation to the next, with little use for history, let alone critical genealogy or practice. In that sense, the chapters in this book do provide a kind of guidebook, although I'd still argue that it is more of a compass and a reveal than a guidebook. We can quibble with each other as you read these offerings, if guidebook as a word, as a concept, is retrievable from the attempted Cartesian split between mind and body and the grip of narratives that pastiche over guidebooks written for encroachment and captivity. I suspect that you won't want to quibble with me about that because there are too many folds and stretches here to linger in, to think about while cooking, while walking, while resting, while grieving, while living.

We will find our way to be with each other in so many of the elegant, resonant moves in this book that Amanda and Z have brilliantly guided with love. Each chapter's citational practices bring educational research into relation with fields and critical genealogies that it has long needed to center humanity, life, possibility, and refusal. As Toni Morrison has taught us, and tries to teach us at every turn, we who are considered at the margins have always been in the center. This volume helps to bring that center into right relation from where we stand and in the shifting spaces that shift because we are unlearning. I wonder if you, like me, will have a more robust understanding of positionality, and more specifically who is asked to name their positionality, as a fixed entity, while you are reading and lingering in these pages. Positionality is always present and always dynamic. Perhaps someday the force of this work and who it invites into conversation will refuse how infrequently positionality is asked of any researcher who crafts findings from inferential statistical research. There is nothing in this book that does not speak to all forms of building and being with knowledge.

For Wayne and I, much of our connected words in these bookends is etched with the deep destabilizations found in several tyrannies rising in and hooking into existing oppressions through the global pandemic. There is no way that I could have found a way to write these words without the grace and deep humanity of K. Wayne Yang. I have been reading his work for years, have been fortunate enough to be in some shared spaces at conferences, and I always learn. Writing these bookends has been no exception. Similarly, I could not have gathered myself to pay attention to the weaving and many places where I encountered loops and twists across place without Amanda and Z's generosity and care for our well-being.

As I think about the ways that we have been with each other in the timing of that writing for this beautiful book, I am drawn back to Arundhati Roy's much quoted essay about pandemics being portals. I won't belabor (too much) if this pandemic has been a portal. It has, and I'm afraid history will continue to document just how heavily many societies chose to drag heavy baggage and disregard connectedness not just through the portal but extending the pandemic with a deep toll. Instead, let's turn to another drop of brilliance in Roy's essay: that things are not getting worse; they are becoming uncovered. The offerings in this book uncover so much possibility when we wrest ourselves away from, refuse, perhaps saunter lightly—you know your own stride at this moment—toward relation and practice. The invitation is to step into relation with ways of knowing, with ourselves, with living beings now, the ghosts trying to have their seeds take root, the babies yet to be born, and of course, always, place.

Research has, in fact, been such a dirty word to so many peoples: Native, Black, queer, disabled, refugee, trans, poor, migrant, usable and discardable in the name of status and property. As Amanda and Z dreamed this book into formation, invited these authors, curated this work, and now invite you and I to be in relation to what is being uncovered, let us do so with the intertwined reverence, truth, and joy that is woven through the words in this book. I don't want to tell you too much about who says what at this early point; I feel I'd be stealing away the surprises that await you, but there is one of many references that I hope you'll find pulls you and at you. One chapter brings in Toni Cade Bambara's words from *The Salt Eaters* to accompany the authors' practices of placemaking in a society that has tried to tell them horrible lies about themselves. As poet and activist Darnell Moore teaches us, we are told lies by societies founded on violence—lies that we come to love, even the ones that try to tell us horrible things about ourselves. In this chapter, these authors functionally and joyfully tell us how they broke up with these lies, with the help and hold of Bambara's words: "You have to be whole to see whole." We must look at and be with what is being uncovered. That gravity and joy will always be waiting for us when we are able to be whole, to see whole in these pages and patterns. Bambara also offered a question in *The Salt Eaters* that echoes across time and space and feels fitting as you step into relation in this book: "Are you sure, sweetheart, that you really want to be well? . . . Just so's you're sure, sweetheart, and ready to be healed. Because wholeness is no trifling matter."

I'll see you in the pages, the patterns, the weaving. We won't trifle. We'll witness. We'll create ways of being and remember the ones who have been waiting for us to return to them. It will be what we've been waiting for because there is no other way to be with this book than through sincerity. So let's get into it, not onward or forward, but toward.

—Leigh Patel

Inspired by my friend and colleague, Wayne Yang, I did not use APA reference style throughout this essay. Here are some of the many works from wise people whose imprints are in these forward/toward:

References

Bambara, T. C. (1992). *The salt eaters*. Vintage.

Dillard, C B. (2011). Learning to remember the things we've learned to forget. In N. K. Denzin & M. D. Giaradina (Eds.), *Qualitative inquiry and global crises* (pp. 226–243). Routledge. https://doi.org/10.4324/9781315421612-12

Grande, S., & McCarty, T. L. (2018). Indigenous elsewheres: Refusal and re-membering in education research, policy, and praxis. *International Journal for Qualitative Studies in Education*, *31*(3), 165–167. https://doi.org/10.1080/09518398.2017.1401144

Moore, D. L. (2018). *No ashes in the fire: Coming of age Black and free in America.* Hachette UK.

Morrison, T. (2020). *Playing in the dark: Whiteness and the literary imagination.* Vintage.

Roy, A. (2020, April 3). The pandemic is a portal. *Financial Times.* https://www.ft.com/content/10d8f5e8-74eb-11ea-95fe-fcd274e920ca

Shalaby, C. (2017). *Troublemakers: Lessons in freedom from young children at school.* The New Press.

Smith, L. T. (2021). *Decolonizing methodologies: Research and indigenous peoples.* Zed Books.

Vizenor, G. (Ed.). (2008). *Survivance: Narratives of native presence.* University of Nebraska Press.

Wa Thiong'o, N. (1992). *Decolonising the mind: The politics of language in African literature.* East African Publishers.

ACKNOWLEDGMENTS

We want to thank the beautiful writers who all graciously accepted our invitation, especially during a time when our world (and our place in it) was (and continues) feeling through the COVID-19 pandemic as well as the ongoing onslaught of racial reckoning.

We want to thank Leigh Patel and K. Wayne Yang, who also accepted our invitation to write the foreword and afterword, as bookends, which in many ways symbolizes, for us, warm hugs embracing our collective text.

We want to thank Stylus Publishing, especially Stylus President John von Knorring, for patiently and persistently connecting with us. We are so thankful to be members of the Stylus author family.

We want to thank Stephen Santa-Ramirez, who invited us onto a panel for the American Educational Research Association that became one of the beginnings for this book.

We want to recognize and give thanks to the lands that held us, nourished us, and allowed us to take care of each other and the ones we love through the writing and editing of this book, including those of the Akimel O'odham and Pee Posh peoples (Phoenix, AZ); the Nichił'ana and the Ninilchik Village Tribe (Homer, AK, the location of the Storyknife Writers Retreat); the Potawatomi, Ottawa, and Ojibway (The People of the Three Fires; Grand Rapids, MI); the Tohono O'odham and Pascua Yaqui peoples (Tucson, AZ); the Chumash, Tongva, Fernandeño Tataviam, and Kizh peoples (Sylmar, CA); and the Diné (Ganado, AZ).

We want to acknowledge and thank our families, without whom none of this would be possible. To those family members who are no longer with us, we feel your presence daily. To those family members who are with us, thank you for all you do each and every day to bring joy to our lives. And to those family members we have yet to meet, we cannot wait to enjoy the days to come and to grow alongside you.

We want to thank our professional families, the people who have always made the academy a softer, more critical, and more deeply engaged space for the two of us. Many of these people have become more than colleagues and are cherished members of our lives. We've celebrated weddings, mourned losses, and enjoyed the mundaneness of weeks with them. We love you and appreciate all you continue to bring to our lives.

We want to thank our pets, Grrtrude and Layla, who continue to bring us so much joy, as well as remind us that work should always take a back seat to running around in the backyard and taking long walks.

We want to thank artists such as textile weavers who help us to imagine an otherwise, and who inspire us to think more expansively about qualitative research.

We want to thank the children (Coral, Brien, Noelle) for your unwavering love, teasing, and strength. In many ways, we weave an otherwise for you.

And of course, we want to give a special shout out to our sweeties, who were by our sides through this process. Big thanks to Brian and Moira, who cleared space for us, brought us snacks and food, and provided love through the entirety of the writing and editing process.

We love you all.

INTRODUCTION

Amanda R. Tachine and Z Nicolazzo

in-tro-duc-tion

noun

1. the action of introducing something.
2. a formal presentation of one person to another, in which each is told the other's name. (Oxford English Dictionary, n.d.)

introduction(s)

Verb, action-oriented, living

3. a greeting (shaking of hands or a head nod; movement of body) that then sequences to a verbal acknowledgement that we are not separate, but that we are in-relations to a long lineage of relatives including kinship relationships and the living land that we are connected to. Sometimes in a language other than English. Depending upon context, location, and company; action differs. Time is not regarded as much because who keeps track of time during introductions? Respect for the relationship is often of preference, but time lurks by. (From Indigenous ways of knowing, passed down from generations to generations, changing and evolving.)

*   *   *   *

There is a reason why you are here, dare we say a purpose for you to grab this book and then open the pages. You may be a doctoral student in the process of thinking through your research, pondering over what to study, where to engage in a question (or questions, ahh!! The many questions!), and considering the methods that align with not just your research design, but also your heart, values, vision, and hopes. Some of you have acquired a doctoral degree and continue to be led to engage in research that moves away from rigidity and tightness that orient us toward prescribed steps that do not fit well with the people and the land we are from and/or want to learn from (Smith, 1999). We get it. We have walked in those same steps and tripped over the trepidations. We have struggled with the constraints and pulls that Eurocentric qualitative research methods impose on our bodies, communities, and futures. We want to be careful and not suggest that all Eurocentric

1

ways are constraining. It is not our intention with this book to argue about the good and bad of research. Rather, we are exploring possibilities by weaving an otherwise in qualitative research. In these pages, we see *weaving an otherwise* as the interconnectedness of storytelling that seeks to pause (Patel, 2016), explore, and deepen an otherwise that honors being in relations with each other, the land, and expansive waterways, and more-than-human beings. We are here to learn together, and we are excited that you are with us, because there is power in knowing that we are not alone; that is the force of an otherwise. Remember that. And there are creative energies in knowing that qualitative methodology can be a resourceful tool for us to align research with our heart, values, visions, and hopes.

We begin by viewing qualitative research methods as, at their best, a series of introductions. They are modes through which scholars share names, present themselves with those engaged in close conversations, as well as doorways through which scholars can invite readers into careful community with possibly new (and old) worlds. Qualitative research methods are also action oriented (a verb), creating threads where we recognize and feel more deeply that we are in relations with life and the world around us. Nothing is solitary, and no one is singular; this is a beautiful gift that qualitative research methods can remind us of time and again. Even the autoethnographer is (hyper)connected to their past/present/future selves, worlds, and communities. These overlaps and overreadings are the very stuff from which we—a constellation of qualitative scholars whose names are weft through the pages of this book you are holding—(continue to) weave this text. That is, even though the ink has dried and set on the pages you read, the text moves with/in/around/through/between (all of) us. We continue to introduce and be introduced each time we come back to the text, with awareness of an ongoing meaning-making process in each turnaround.

Introductions can never be separated from place, *or can they?* They cannot be separated from the broader movements and social location(s) that influence their happenings and are made richer by getting closer to the *where, when, how,* and *why* of their becomings. Introductions, as a verb, make more sense when one pays attention to senses: the smell, feel, sound, intuition, and sight—the visual sensorium as it exists beyond the fallacious notion that one only sees with their eyes—of introductions matter. The wisdom of sensory fields in and through which introductions occur encourage depth and promote intimacies. In this sense, then, it is important that we (Amanda and Z) share the places from which this text came to be (and continues to become). In phases of life, we shifted across gender becomings, changing milestones and achievements, and familial roles. We recognized the multiple unfolding iterations of ourselves and relationships to one another. One telling is that it *began* with a presentation on decolonizing methods at the 2019 American Educational Research Association's annual meeting. Both of us were invited to speak, after which we were approached about developing ideas into an edited text. Another telling is that it continues to unfold *during* a time of unfathomable upheaval, rising out of a pandemic and concurrent social, economic, racial, and political reckonings that continue to exert extreme tolls on (all of) our lives, author and reader alike. Both of us (Amanda and Z) processed grief and trauma through the seasons this text shaped, and bore witness, held space, and felt alongside as chapter authors experienced the same. We thought about how, months ago, Amanda's contact information changed to show up in Z's phone as Mom Tachine, and that small (yet profound) connection between Amanda and her children coincided with Z's connection with her beautiful mother, all in seasons of deep loss of close loved ones. Yet another telling is that it takes place in the *after*ward, the space between us as authors and you as readers, in the contours, crevices, and textures we stretch to dream alongside each other. *Sharing our names (and evolution) creates a tapestry, a rich interconnected reality in which we (each of us) move from being singular to plural (both/all of us) through our thinking, sharing, being together across worlds. We think of all the wonderful ways we will get to keep experiencing and exercising introductions for years to come.*

And the thing is, all of these becomings make sense. All of them tell us things about both the text and ourselves, and what we can do to imagine, dream, desire, and envision freedom, which we understand as a process of becoming rather than a permanent utopic state (which may not exist, which need not exist, which we desire to will to exist). la paperson (2017) stated that a more liberatory university is "anti-utopian. . . . A third world university is less interested in decolonizing the university and more in operating as a decolonizing university" (p. 10). *We then arrive with the knowledge that our coming together was more significant than a chance encounter. Possibly it was predetermined, already written.*

We recognize that qualitative research methods produce, at their best, disruption and then a process of re-warping. They encourage unsettling un/realities through which we can question that which we (think we) have come to know. They remind us of the power of dreaming, of weaving the worlds we need, of demanding for that which the state codifies as excessive, as if excess was a pejorative mode of being. This text is, then, a site of disruption, is intended to prick and prod the un/conscious, and to move (all of) us to move, together. We seek not to reform qualitative research methods through this text, but to gesture toward a refusal (Simpson, 2007) of those traditions in which qualitative research methods have become an invasive species, choking back possibilities from blooming. Qualitative research methods can re/produce blooms aplenty, quite like those of the tulips, daffodils, fireweed, cotton grass, and ocotillo that ripple across the lands as we (Amanda and Z) draft these very words.

*   *   *   *

Stol:lo and Coast Salish scholar Jo-Ann Archibald (2008) Q'um Q'um Xiiiem gifted us with her beautiful methodology of *Indigenous Storywork: Educating the Heart, Mind, and Spirit*, which is an Indigenous theoretical, methodological, and pedagogical framework that comprises seven principles: respect, responsibility, reverence, reciprocity, holism, interrelatedness, and synergy. Indigenous storywork served as an ethical guide and a meaning-making process for researchers (Archibald et al., 2019) that underscores the power of interrelatedness to oneself, family, land/waterways, and the wider universe. While Amanda was in the dissertation process, her mentor Dr. Jenny Lee introduced *Indigenous Storywork* to Amanda, and she was forever deeply moved and changed. "I felt like the book was talking directly to me." Learning from Archibald provided a sense of freedom to assert Diné ways into research methodology as Eurocentric ways of research were not adequately fitting. Amanda was inspired to see, feel, and then develop methodological work as a *story rug* (Tachine, 2015, 2022) that built off of storywork and engaged in Diné ways of weaving. In Robin Starr Minthorn and Heather J. Shotton's (2018) book titled *Reclaiming Indigenous Research in Higher Education,* Amanda wrote a chapter about the development of a story rug as an Indigenous research framework. She described the setting up of the loom and gathering of weaving tools, the warping and weaving process, and taking the rug off of the loom. While broad phases of weaving were explored, she connected that process to setting up a research design, including writing the literature review, framing the methods, gathering the data (stories) into findings, and providing discussion and implications. Since that publication, she continues to learn, write, and work her hands through the warps and wefts of the weaving loom to expand on the story rug as not only a framework, but as a rigorous analytical tool, as methodology.

In weaving, the loom can teach us that research is active, that it requires movement and rest, and that it recognizes that knowledge does not solely derive from human knowledge but includes more than human (land and Spider Woman) wisdom and knowledges that are often tangled and twisted, which requires our utmost presence, patience, and humility. Pueblo researcher Anya Dozier Enos (2017) shared spider webs as a "messy" methodology that attends to the ways that this work is not easy nor prescribed:

> to think through gathering information, how relationships and concepts interrelate and then how those ideas are shared and used, meaning going back and forth between how to gather information, and then how to

analyze, present and use the findings with the goal of benefitting Pueblo community. This is not neatly predictable or organized; it is the messiness of research that results in something powerful. It is the spider web. (p. 42)

Spider webs are much like weaving textiles, especially given that Spider Woman taught Diné people how to weave. These teachings of messiness and cohesion help develop the analytical process of weaving stories and display them in a patterned way.

Spider webs, messiness, and cohesion are the woven practice ways that tie qualitative research into beautiful tapestries. Stories are threaded throughout the weft and warps of each turnaround that brings us closer and closer to the intimacies of relationality and visions of otherwise worlds that create living textiles of past, present and future worlds. You see, we are weavers connected to stories and lives that are not absent from sociopolitical realities of injustices. In our weaving process, we feel the threads of hurt, tension, and pain because what one feels is connected to another and another. We are not separate, but intimately threaded together. While we tamp down and connect stories and see our intertwined connections with ourselves and the world around us, we then continue another turnaround for survivance (Vizenor, 1994), love, and hope. That is the foundation of this book.

We are releasing the shackles of how we think research should be done that is devoid from our ways of being.

We are wondering about how we can weave an otherwise for the future.

We are grabbing your hand and welcoming you to this venture with us, because you are not alone; we are in this together.

Won't you come with us?

*   *   *   *

We have divided this text into three phases (before, during, and after) to illustrate the weaving as an otherwise process that is reflective of Diné textile weaving practices. In what follows, we discuss each of the three sections, as well as the chapter offerings in them. We then conclude our introduction with a continued invitation to join us and the chapter authors to weave an otherwise through qualitative research.

Before

The first section of the text is titled "Before" as a signal to what must be done in advance of one's weaving on the loom. The *beginning* process takes into account the essential and laborious task of placing and stretching warp yarns on a loom, in order to secure a tight and readied foundation. The warping process is important for the weaver and the textile, as the pausing, coming to know, and strengthening of relationality are occurring. These moments of pausing, reflection, and intentionality are also all vital concepts in research. What moves us toward our research? What scares us about the work we may undergo? How are we always in and of our work, and how must we be clear about what that means for what we coproduce alongside the participants with whom we are in community? These (and many other) questions signal a before temporality, a beginning and setting up that is essential to the overall qualitative research process. As such, contributions in this section of the book think through various concepts that influence how we pause, think about, feel through, and come to our study designs as qualitative researchers, as we start the laborious task of warping our research.

In the first chapter Samuel D. Museus and Amy C. Wang provide an important refusal to the press of neoliberalism in the academy. Centering reflexivity, responsibility, and relationships, the authors ask, "What does research design look like when human connections are central to, rather than stripped from, it?" The authors provide a necessary intervention, reimagining the various harms and violences of a detached and restrictive research process as one that could—and perhaps more emphatically stated, *should*—be imbued with connectedness, relationality, and humanity. As the authors detail through their chapter, although we may never be able to get fully out from the tangles of neoliberalism, we can certainly refuse the conditions through which it insists upon separation, individualism, and scarcity illogics.

In the second chapter, Leilani Sabzalian and Angie Morrill open with an art exhibit from Natalie Ball (Black/Modoc/Klamath). Sabzalian and Morrill share Ball's artist statement for the exhibit, titled "We Have Teeth Too," in which she chillingly states, "It's not enough to be dead, you want us murdered. It's not enough to be murdered, you want us dismembered. It's not enough to be in pieces, you want us stolen. And then forgotten." Thinking alongside Ball, the authors bring readers into deep conversation about survivance as a mode of being, thinking, and feeling qualitative research. Sabzalian and Morrill also share their own survivance stories, inviting readers into a storying of Indigenous life, providing a way to understand survivance as both qualitative method/ology and affirmation that Indigenous life has, does, and will thrive through the violences of settler coloniality.

In the final chapter for this section, Reginald Blockett, Leonard Taylor Jr., and Steve D. Mobley Jr. invite readers into an intimate glimpse into their onto-epistemological kinship formation they refer to as Bella Noche's. Here, Blockett, Taylor Jr., and Mobley Jr. explore the methodological, affective, and material dimensions of kinship, reminding us all of how these comings together are always already infused with practices of Black-queer world-making. In so doing, the authors signal how race/gender/sexuality is deeply present through research, life, and researching life, a totalizing presence with which they encourage us to listen, feel, and move as qualitative researchers.

During

The second section of this text is titled "During." In relation to the weaving process, the *during* phase places emphasis on being in relation to the textile, loom, and environment that seeks to weave beyond conventional patterns and pathways. It is in this present tense, the ongoing nowness, through which qualitative researchers create research that recognizes the interconnectedness that began in the before, in the pauses and reflective moments that previously occurred. Here, one can get a sense of how the during weaves into the before, creating a tapestry that binds, connects, and draws together and near. It is not that interconnectedness was not previously present in body/mind/spirit, but that connection becomes central to the weaving of qualitative research in this temporal phase. Honoring this research moment, contributors in this section of the book seek to weave beyond conventional patterns and pathways that create research that recognizes and centers interconnectedness knowledge.

The fourth chapter, and the first of this second section of the book, welcomes an understanding of Kazanjian's (2015) methodological practice of overreading. In his chapter, Zachary Brown uses one photograph, an archival image of the 1968–1969 San Francisco State College protests, to create excessive understandings of archival research and its varied im/possibilities. That is, Brown seeks to push on how archives desire to create articulations of Black socialites rooted in anti-Black notions of humanity/the human, and as a result provides a delicious rendering of how overreading as a methodological approach can de/re/construct multiple, shifting futurescapes for Black liberatory praxis.

Irene H. Yoon and Grace A. Chen's chapter implores readers on the importance of witnessing the absent presences that haunt qualitative research. That is, Yoon and Chen remark on the affective and effective nature of ghosts, prodding readers to re/think if, as the overly simplistic idiom suggests, seeing is believing. By heeding hauntings—both the authors' specific renderings and the broader movements of ghosts/ghosting through qualitative research—Yoon and Chen use a promiscuous stitching of sources and storying styles as a way to create openings for the complexity of historicized beings with futures and freedom dreams.

In chapter 6, Chris A. Nelson and Heather J. Shotton discuss gifting as a way to understand the notion of answerability. Using poetry as a storying practice, Nelson and Shotton tussle with three vital questions: "To whom do we answer when we engage in our research? To what and for what knowledge and teachings are we responsible? How do we engage in a praxis of answerability?" In their offering, the gift is imbued with meaning and being, becoming both a symbol and practice through which gifting/Gift unravels otherwise possibilities for decolonizing qualitative research, and as a result, moving into right relationships with oneself as well as other people, the land, and more-than-human species.

After

After the warping process (*before*), and the textile has been woven (*during*), the textile is ready to be taken off the loom and to have its beauty shared. This moment is not separate from, but is an integral part of the weaving process. That is, to share, to be in community, to bring (closer) together, and to revisit the textile so as to learn again (and again) from what one has created are important parts of the overall weaving process. These moments make up the practice of world-making that stretches forward and moves us toward imagining otherwises and elsewheres. In linking weaving to the qualitative research process, it is in these after moments that researchers, participants, and readers alike, linked through the before and during phases of research, can imagine, desire, and call into being the worlds we need and want. In this way, qualitative research as weaving becomes a practice of critical hope, one in which we are bonded together in creating full and rich pasts/presents/futures. Signaling the praxis of world-making, these chapter offerings in this section create openings for researchers and readers alike to imagine the yet to be by stretching beyond the worlds we are taught are given, immutable, natural (as in a static misunderstanding by which what is will always be).

In the first chapter of the text's final section, Keon M. McGuire, Kirsten T. Edwards, and T. Elon Dancy II think solidarity through Blacklove. That is, the authors envision Blacklove as fundamental to one's reorientation toward possibilities for sociality within/alongside research, as well as for being clear about the stakes of such practices of vulnerability. Wrapped through narratives highlighting the entangled realities of gender/sexuality/race, the authors move between individual and collective storytelling to imagine Blacklove in relation to qualitative methodology.

Next, Kyle Halle-Erby and Harper Keenan envision abolition as a set of fugitive practices that require qualitative researchers to reimagine their orientations toward education(al institutions). Describing themselves as "students of abolition," Halle-Erby and Keenan draw from lineages of queer, trans, Black, and Indigenous activists/scholars/dreamers to imagine possibilities for what abolition means in and beyond the academy. Moreover, the authors share excerpts from conversations with abolitionist organizers, teachers, and researchers in the hopes of "shap[ing] the methodological commitments of other students of abolition and contribut[ing] to a material practice of political imagination within educational research."

The final chapter for this book, "Gesturing Towards Decolonial Futures Collective," a research/arts/ecology collective comprising 23 "researchers, artists, educators, students, social justice and environmental activists, and Indigenous knowledge keepers," invites readers to understand decolonization as an ongoing practice of un/re/learning. Outlining what they refer to as the bus methodology, the collective offer a model by which to explore the complex affective traces that mediate decoloniality. They end with hyper–self-reflexivity questions, marking how we are—as we must be—implicated in developing the presents/futures we desire and need.

*   *   *   *

Readers will also note this text is bookended with a foreword by Leigh Patel and an afterword by K. Wayne Yang. As dreamers ourselves, we (Amanda and Z) are deeply grateful to these two scholars, colleagues, and friends who provide our texts with openings. In a sense, both the foreword and afterword act as escape hatches to otherwise worlds. Put another way, Patel and Yang provide glimpses into that which could be, may yet become, and always already exists in various modes that can never be captured by ossified ways of knowing, against which we hope this text provides relief. Similar to how Kaba (2021) notes abolition is both a horizon and also being lived in the present tense, Patel and Yang offer ways of envisioning the qualitative landscapes we need in the future through that which is happening in the here and now.

Sitting at the Loom: In Relations Methodological Practice

Like introductions, qualitative research is not just a doing. The process and practice of qualitative research weaves together the temporal, spatial, and affective, making something more than was once thought possible. Like introductions, qualitative research is not a solitary process. Even if only one person is listed as the researcher, we are always in relation to and with various communities—past, present, and future; land-based, human, and more than human—as we envision the worlds we need and want. Not only is the research process *a source* of (inter)connection, but the process itself is *developed through* (inter)connection. In this way, then, qualitative research can be a profound space/time/feeling through which we weave otherwises. It is these profuse possibilities that we and the chapter authors introduce throughout this book that you are holding now.

Sometimes, too, introductions are a space of revisiting, revising, and coming together again. As we talked about previously, our (Amanda and Z) relationship has spanned multiple introductions across gender, family orientation, and connections to land. While we have "known each other" for over a decade, we have continued to hold open space and time to meet each other anew, over and over again. Similar to the qualitative research method(ologie)s chapter contributors discuss in this book, we invite you, our readers, to sit at the loom with us over and over again. Maybe you will read a chapter that will challenge you, that will provoke and prod your curiosities, that will animate your senses. Maybe you will need to move away from the book because you have other things going on, or someone is calling, or you need to make dinner. But we hope you will come back, will introduce yourself to us as editors and chapter contributors, and will be open to our introducing ourselves, over and over again. For, as we wrote at the beginning of this chapter,

> introduction(s) (from Indigenous ways of knowing, passed down from generations to generations, changing and evolving)
>
> *Verb, action-oriented, living*
>
> 3. a greeting (shaking of hands or a head nod; movement of body) that then sequences to a verbal acknowledgement that we are not separate, but that we are in-relations to a long lineage of relatives including kinship relationships and the living land that we are connected to. Sometimes in a language other than English. Depending upon context, location, and company; action differs. Time is not regarded as much because who keeps track of time during introductions? Respect for the relationship is often of preference, but time lurks by. (Oxford English Dictionary, n.d.)

We look forward to sitting, resting, thinking, and feeling with you by the loom, weaving otherwises through qualitative research. Won't you come with us?

References

Archibald, J. (2008). *Indigenous storywork: Educating the heart, mind, body, and spirit.* UBC Press.

Archibald, J., Lee-Morgan, J. B. J., & De Santolo, J. (2019). *Decolonizing research: Indigenous storywork as methodology.* ZED Books.

Dozier Enos, A. (2017). With respect. . . . In E. S. Hauman & B. M. J. Brayboy (Eds.), *Indigenous innovations in higher education* (pp. 41–57). Sense.

Kaba, M. (2021). *We do this 'til we free us: Abolitionist organizing and transforming justice.* Haymarket Books.

Kazanjian, D. (2015). Scenes of speculation. *Social Text, 125,* 77–84. https://doi .org/10.1215/01642472-3315778

la paperson. (2017). *A third university is possible.* University of Minnesota Press.

Minthorn, R., & Shotton, H. (2018). *Reclaiming Indigenous research in higher education.* Rutgers University Press.

Oxford University Press. (n.d.) Introduction. *Oxford English dictionary.*

Patel, L. (2016). *Decolonizing educational research: From ownership to answerability.* Routledge.

Simpson. A. (2007). On ethnographic refusal: Indigeneity, "voice" and colonial citizenship. *Junctures,* (9), 67–80. https://link.gale.com/apps/doc/A176129665/ AONE?u=anon-c74fed77&sid=googleScholar&xid=1fd34580

Smith, L. T. (1999). *Decolonizing methodologies: Research and Indigenous peoples.* ZED Books.

Tachine, A. R. (2015). *Monsters and weapons: Navajo students' stories on their journeys toward college* (Order No. 3704874) [Doctoral dissertation, University of Arizona]. ProQuest.

Tachine, A. R. (2022). *Native presence and sovereignty in college: Sustaining Indigenous weapons to defeat systemic monsters.* Teachers College Press.

Vizenor, G. (1994). *Manifest manners: Post-Indian warriors of survivance.* University of Nebraska Press.

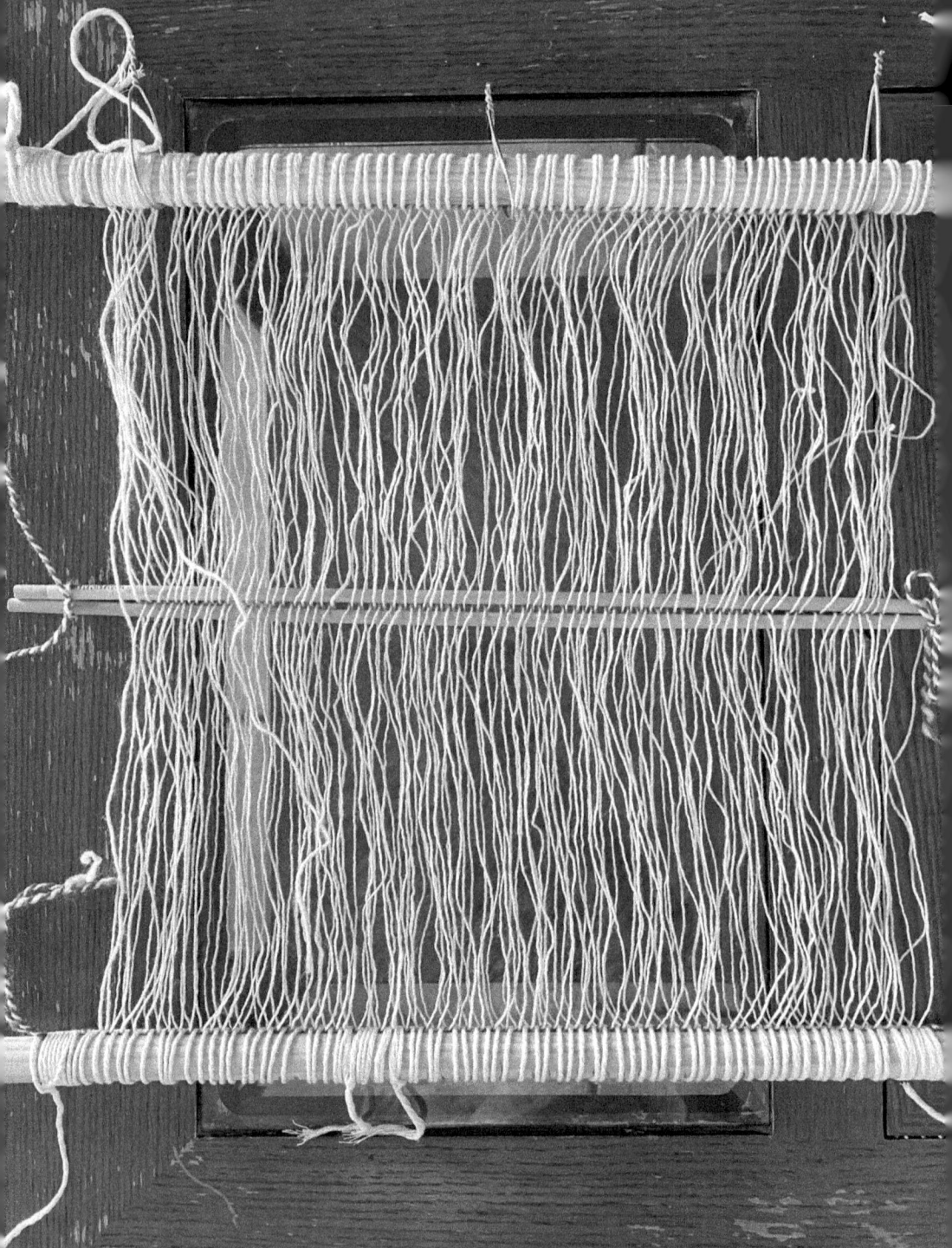

PART ONE

BEFORE

REFUSING NEOLIBERAL LOGICS IN RESEARCH DESIGN

Samuel D. Museus and Amy C. Wang

Like many people, I was seduced by the opportunity to pursue research with my communities to advocate positive change in society. The passion to advocate with these communities drove me into my doctoral program, eager to learn how to conduct research that could advance their cause. I took research methods courses in graduate school that were taught by prominent scholars in the field. I learned how to select methodological approaches to answer research questions, design rigorous empirical inquiries, utilize various data collection and analysis techniques, and of course navigate IRB processes. We were taught that these tools were what we needed to contribute to knowledge that would serve our communities.

Aspects of the research process with which I would grapple the most throughout my career were completely absent from the methods curriculum. After I became a faculty member, I would have to navigate the politics of competition in social justice scholarly circles and the complexities of working with diverse communities whose histories and political agendas heavily shaped the ways I could and did work with them through research processes. While we had courses that dealt with issues directly related to diverse communities, the curriculum did not provide space to learn about the moral issues that arise when researching with them. While graduate school served me in many ways, it left me ill-equipped to deal with these human dynamics of research, which were ignored so we could consume all of the tools and techniques necessary to carry out concrete tasks and maximize our "productivity" after graduation.

—Sam

Scholars at the margins have lived with tangible systemic violence that harms real lives in the communities that they love. The desire to disrupt the destruction of human lives and the environment, which we use to refer to Indigenous land and waterways, drives many to pursue academic careers, and it also sustains them. It should come as no surprise that many graduate programs fail to center these elements of the research process. After all, the academy is extremely effective and efficient at stripping people and things of their humanity (Museus, 2020). Within scholarly research, academic cultures bombard people with messages that they must focus on the rapid production of quantifiable things over what is best for people and environment (Gonzales & Núñez, 2014).

What does research design look like when human connections are central to, rather than stripped from, it? We invite you to imagine the possibilities with us. The purpose of this chapter is twofold. First, we critique the ways in which the current culture of academia is a process of inculcating settler colonial and neoliberal logics that encourage scholars to dehumanize the research process. In addition, we discuss how we grapple with concepts of reflexivity, responsibility, and relationships. We believe that such critical questions might help infuse humanity throughout its research endeavors.

Settler Colonialism, Neoliberalism, and Academic Capitalism

Patrick Wolfe (1999) explains that settler colonialism is an existing and evolving structure founded upon the removal of Indigenous peoples from land as a precondition of settlement. In settler colonial states, settlers have aimed "to control space, resources, and people not only by occupying land but also by establishing an exclusionary private property regime and coercive labor systems, including chattel slavery to work the land, extract resources, and build infrastructure" (Glenn, 2015, p. 52). Therefore, settler colonialism is founded on the theft of Indigenous land and pervasive logics of Native erasure (la paperson, 2017).

Settler colonialism and neoliberalism are inextricably intertwined (Lloyd & Wolfe, 2016), and the latter makes the contours of the former more apparent (Grande, 2018). Settler colonialism is fueled by desires to steal, accumulate, and exploit Indigenous land for national economic gain. Neoliberalism has become the dominant political logic around the globe and demands an ever-expanding exploitation of people, land, and water to accumulate capital and redistribute it into the hands of the corporate elite (Lloyd & Wolfe, 2016). To realize this exploitation, neoliberalism seeks to individualize all communities, assimilate them into the neoliberal political economy, and remove Indigenous communities from the land.

Neoliberalism is a market-driven political logic that permeates societies in the United States and around the globe (Brown, 2006). There is no single definition of neoliberalism, but literature critiquing it consistently highlights several common elements (Museus & LePeau, 2019). First, neoliberalism infuses consumerism throughout society and fuels a culture where the potential revenue that people and things are capable of producing determines their value. Second, neoliberalism is grounded in values of hyper-competition and false meritocracy, encouraging people to prioritize their own individual self-interest to survive and maximize their accumulation of resources and eroding community. Third, neoliberal forces create and infuse systems of surveillance (e.g., monitoring and reporting) throughout society to guarantee people comply with neoliberal rationalities, which erode trust. Fourth, neoliberal systems provide people with limited resources and place fiscal responsibility on individuals, ensuring perpetual precarity that treats people as expendable and pressures them to fight for their own survival. Finally, neoliberal systems shift energy away from declining moral imperatives and pressure people to constantly focus their energies and efforts on capital accumulation (Museus & LePeau, 2019).

Neoliberalism is reshaping institutions of higher education into increasingly entrepreneurial organizations. Writing about academic capitalism, Sheila Slaughter and Gary Rhoades (2004) detail the ways in which neoliberalism has influenced how institutions of higher education function, but they also underscore how colleges and universities have become active players in reinforcing neoliberal logics and reinscribing them throughout the higher education system. These processes also reinforce the universities' continued occupation of Indigenous land, exploitation of human resources to work the land, and continued efforts to accumulate more stolen land and capital at the expense of Indigenous communities.

It is difficult to find spaces or environments on college campuses that are not infected with neoliberal rationalities in some way, shape, or form. As a result, scholars' socialization into academia has largely become socialization into the neoliberal order (Harney & Moton, 2013). This socialization into the neoliberal knowledge economy also acts as a process of researchers becoming tools to be exploited by the settler state and university.

In the following sections, we utilize personal narratives to highlight how we grapple with becoming a tool of the neoliberal university, and therefore the settler state, and engage the reader in considering the implications of these stories. In doing so, we use the term *we* to refer to the authors and *you* to reference the reader. However, it is important to note that everything we say to "you," we have said to ourselves, as we are all a part of this system.

The Neoliberal Machine and Socialization Into Academic Research

In one course, we devoted the entire term to writing drafts of a dissertation fellowship application for a large foundation. I remember having mixed emotions, ranging from excitement to dread. Initially, I was grateful for an opportunity to sit down and think through my proposal in ways that could lead to funding, which I so desperately need as a graduate student. The overwhelming fear of failure came over me. What if I am not good enough? What if they do not find it interesting? What if they think the topic is not important? Still, I was excited to spend our class preparing applications for a renowned award that this scholar and that scholar won. I began to wonder how I can make myself more enticing, my work more cutting-edge, and my problem statement more dramatic.

By the third iteration of the proposal, I realized I was not prioritizing my ideas or writing for myself. Instead, I absorbed the metrics put forth by the foundation and was spending a significant amount of time reading unrelated studies just to make sure that my proposal was as unique as I claimed it to be. For instance, I changed my explanation of why a particular method aligned with my study to an extensive soliloquy of how this method was cutting-edge to my field of study and no one was doing this work. What I had in front of me was not just a proposal, it was a manifestation of my fears and anxieties around academic precarity, competition, and market desires. When I realized I had lost my original train of thought, I saw my proposal got worse and was misaligned in several areas because I had been so concerned with showing off and trying to "win."

—Amy

As you come into the academy with a primary emphasis on advocating with the oppressed and advancing moral causes, you are quickly socialized into shifting your energy toward generating external revenue, fighting for lead authorship for maximum credit, accumulating prestige through publishing a maximum number of articles in top-tier journals, and optimizing your visibility via social media branding and self-promotion measured through the number of likes and retweets. The desire to optimally perform according to these metrics is also supposed to shape the work you choose to pursue and the ways you design and execute research.

Your socialization into academic research has pressured you to adopt neoliberal logics. You are taught that it is ideal if you can meet the ever-increasing standards and expectations at warp speed to maximize output and return on your investments of time and energy, leaving little room for continuous reflection that is so important in your decolonizing and justice work. In turn, the combined rapid-fire pace and absence of reflection create conditions that are ripe for you to adopt hyper-competitive logics that you are taught will increase your marketability, maximize your professional mobility, and minimize your precarity.

You are also trained to think of research as primarily an individual endeavor, even if you sometimes work with other people. After all, you will be evaluated as an individual for jobs, performance, promotion, and tenure. Even when collaboration is encouraged, the neoliberal machine asserts that you should only engage if you see direct benefits to you that outweigh the additional time required to make collaboration deep and meaningful. The academy conditions you to believe that time and energy spent on things like building genuine relationships and community will undermine your professional goals. In some cases, the systemic pressures to play the neoliberal game and beat everyone in it might become so overwhelming that they reshape your perspectives and become the dominant force shaping your approaches and actions.

You cannot disentangle yourself from the academy while you are situated within it. You cannot divorce, excuse yourself from, or "resist" the neoliberal structures, discourse, and logics shaping your scholarly communities, constantly measuring you, and determining your futures in the academy. However, knowing that you are situated within the neoliberal machine can make it more possible to acknowledge that academic researchers can pursue equity while simultaneously reproducing the technologies that stem from the neoliberal apparatus. Acknowledging that the knowledge economy is an arm of the neoliberal regime within the settler state might make it more likely that you will refuse the neoliberal machine and its logics.

The Neoliberal Paradox and Refusing Neoliberal Logics

How many articles do you have now?

How many do you have in the pipeline?

How many does your institution require for tenure?

How many things are you presenting this year!?

You going to get that early career award?

When I began the tenure track, I began receiving pressures to think about metrics that never consumed my intellectual energy before. I recall being pressured to constantly think about numbers of publications, order of authorship and how much credit researchers were being given for their contributions, and the number of citations I had accrued. I also remember most of my conversations at national conferences revolving around how many papers we were presenting at the convention, how many articles we had produced, how many publications our institutions expected us to publish to get tenure, and who was receiving national awards for their scholarship. The general tone of the discourse was consistently that we all needed to be doing more, and everyone should be aiming for awards that will validate them and prove their worth.

During these pre-tenured years, almost never did I have the opportunity to participate in conversations about the ways in which we were pressured to shift our attention away from doing the most transformative work possible to maximizing our outputs and visibility. In this world, doing transformative work and maximizing outputs became one in the same. This context led to many of us deeply internalizing neoliberal rationalities and turning us into parts of the machine. If this happens, we continue to unapologetically reinforce and spread these logics until we confront them.

—Sam

This clash between neoliberal socialization and the moral values that propelled many of you to enter academia creates what we sometimes refer to as a neoliberal paradox. The notion of a paradox centers on how these forms of socialization reinforce the notion that you can do equity work, as long as you do it according to the neoliberal regime's rules and help spread the same logics that have decimated and subjugated marginalized communities. You can advocate with your communities, but you must do so through hyper-competition with them. You can conduct research on issues most relevant to the communities you love, as long as you do so by standards that they did not define and publish the findings in journals they will never read. You can try to have a positive impact on your communities, as long as doing so does not shift your gaze too far from the superficial quantifiable metrics that your institution's surveillance systems prioritize. At some point in your careers, some of you will question whether the positive impact you sought to have by entering the academy is even possible when it requires you to spend so much of your time feeding the systems that you seek to eradicate.

A silver lining to this dark cloud is the fact that many people in the academy are becoming increasingly impatient with these problems, and there are growing conversations regarding how to refuse dehumanizing neoliberal logics in our work and subvert the machine. Such efforts can benefit from a realistic recognition that the neoliberal regime has already taken over the structures of our professional associations and college campuses. Neoliberal logics shape the construction of space at national conferences, national association and university award processes, and reward systems (e.g., merit, promotion, and tenure reviews). Such acknowledgement might enable the development of mechanisms to refuse the neoliberal turn in academia while navigating the cultures that have sprung from it.

Scholars might benefit from a realistic recognition that the neoliberal regime efficiently infects our minds and worldviews. Writing about feminism, bell hooks (2000) discussed how feminist scholars and activists are hindered by their unwillingness to confront the enemy within, a phrase that she used to describe internalized sexism among women. While hooks focused on sexism, the internalization of oppressive logics among its victims is vital to any discussion about systemic violence. Have you ever found yourself spending more time than you ever wanted to spend thinking about how to out-do people who do work similar to yours? Have you ever been emotionally impacted by how many retweets and likes you received? Do you ever feel pressured to share every accomplishment on Facebook or Twitter? Have you ever wondered why these things have consumed more of your intellectual energy than those that have tangible effects on the human lives or land and waterways you seek to protect? If you are a part of the academy, then you have likely been an active participant in reinforcing these logics (Gildersleeve, 2017).

Oppression is only sustainable if both the privileged and oppressed are convinced that the system works for them (Gramsci, 1971). Many of you have probably been taught that neoliberal ideologies are what is best for us all or is necessary, despite this being far from the truth. Once you have adopted these logics, they are a part of you. Even if you are aware of them and try to unlearn them, they might always be there, waiting to take over. While recognizing and acknowledging the pervasiveness of neoliberalism is necessary to move forward, it is not enough. The awareness of our neoliberal selves can be liberating and open up conversations about refusing neoliberal logics in our beliefs, interactions, and advocacy.

Contemplating Refusal Through Reflexivity, Responsibility, and Relationships

Based on the Haudenosaunee's, and more specifically the Mohawk's, continuous refusal of colonial Canadian and U.S. pressures and notions that such refusals are central to Indigenous nationhood, Audra Simpson (2014) advocates a politic of refusal. Building on Simpson's work, Sandy Grande (2018) explains that settler states consistently seek to entice Indigenous peoples to consent to their own dispossession through individualized inducements. She underscores the need to refuse the individualism that stems from settler neoliberal logics and permeates the academy:

> [It is] a refusal of the cycle of individualized inducements—particularly, the awards, appointments, and grants that require complicity or allegiance to institutions that continue to oppress and dispossess. It is also a call to refuse the perceived imperative to self-promote, to brand one's work and body. This includes all the personal webpages, incessant Facebook updates, and Twitter feeds featuring our latest accomplishments, publications, grants, rewards, etc. etc. Just. Make. It. Stop. The journey is not about self—which means it is not about promotion and tenure—it is about the disruption and dismantling of those structures and processes that create hierarchies of individual worth and labor. (p. 61)

Grande refuses these logics by centering and committing to collectivism (centering community), reciprocity (being responsible to communities we serve), and mutuality (commitments to land and intergenerational resurgence to protect it) in her work. Other scholars demonstrate how they refuse settler logics through centering Indigenous cultural values (Ambo, 2018; Chandler, 2018). We engage these forms of refusal to contribute to conversations about the limitations of neoliberal logics and create opportunity to pause, reflect deeply on our thoughts and emotions that stem from oppressive logics, and imagine new possibilities.

What does research design look like if the desire to refuse settler neoliberal logics is centered in it? We do not have absolute answers, but invite you into our world to collectively grapple with this question. In the following section, we share a series of conversations from our advisor–advisee relationship. Utilizing these dialogues, we contemplate refusing these logics through reflexivity, responsibility, and relationality.

Seeing Reflexivity as Transformative

In education research, the practice of reflexivity is often seen as a mechanism to ensure that the research process and its outcomes do not misrepresent the realities of participants or data collected. In contrast, feminist researchers, such as Kim England (1994), have highlighted the ways in which reflexivity can be transformative, mainly focusing on how it is deployed in scholarly inquiry and within the boundaries of research projects. This scholarship

shows how reflexivity can help researchers better understand their position-
alities in relation to communities with which they work, so that they might
conduct research in more equitable ways.

> Amy: I'm having a really hard time writing my dissertation proposal
> right now. I am at a place where I understand what my role is
> and the power I wield but am unsure about how to talk about
> my hopes to alter traditional research–participant relations and
> dynamics. I think it could be a great opportunity for them to
> do more than share their experiences but also talk about what
> changes they want to see.
>
> Sam: I'm so glad you are grappling with these issues. I think we often
> think about researcher reflexivity as something that is about you
> and your relationship to the work, but it doesn't have to be that
> way. There are a lot of questions that might be useful in re-envi-
> sioning the role of reflexivity—such as, how might reflexivity be
> engaged to facilitate your own transformation as well as that of
> the participants? What, if any, new possibilities arise if you view
> the participants as partners in the project in the process of radical
> imagination and liberation?
>
> Amy: This is really helpful. With research design, I often times think
> we spend a lot of time focusing on what our capacities are as the
> researcher to excavate the participants' stories. This urgency to
> maximize or be "efficient" with your time and energy can prevent
> making space for participants to share what they want from the
> research. I am thinking now about how this project can be a space
> where our hopes and dreams can come together and meet.

Through our conversation, we acknowledge that research often reinforces
settler neoliberal logics. Amy is fearful of designing an inquiry that simply
extracts knowledge from historically oppressed communities for neoliberal
production. In response, Sam asks whether and how reflexivity can serve
as a potential channel to engage in reflective analysis and collective struggle
with participants. We are processing the potential methodological power that
reflexivity can have through serving as a mechanism to leverage in refusal.

Many researchers still do not have or take the time to meaningfully
embed reflexivity into the foundations of the inquiry process. Researchers
often assume reflexivity happens naturally, or they will engage in reflexive
analysis at the end of the research process in order to retroactively understand
how positionality may have shaped the inquiry. If reflexivity is viewed as a
mechanism for positive self-transformation rather than just a technique that

allows one to execute research and generate the necessary deliverables, its impact might not be constrained by the boundaries of a scholarly project. What does reflexivity look like if researchers leverage it to understand how all elements of research processes might be sites of refusal?

You can unlearn the practice of reflexivity as the academy teaches it. It does not have to be a tool that optimizes objective extraction of knowledge from communities. Rather, you can consider research as a vehicle to engage in reflexive struggle and transformation. If you take up the task of continuous reflexivity to understand how neoliberal forces shape your research, then it might create space and opportunities to foster positive self-transformation. You might also realize the potential power of reflexivity as a mechanism of refusal.

Prioritizing Responsibility to Our Communities

It is fairly common to hear researchers talk about their desire to have a positive impact on their communities in interview processes, conference presentations, or personal narratives. It is often assumed that we have a shared understanding regarding what constitutes a positive impact. In reality, there is no consensus regarding what constitutes a positive impact. For example, some might design research to have a positive impact through "giving voice" to communities without access to scholarly publication outlets, but centering voices from our community members in research findings does not preclude us from exploiting them (Lather, 1991). What exactly constitutes a positive impact is subjective, and how we conceptualize impact might have significant implications for thinking about refusal in research design processes.

> Amy: Thanks for meeting with me. I really needed someone to process with. Basically, in class we were discussing the different paradigms in educational research and their utility, and someone asked if there was a list of good frameworks for decolonization and social justice research. I replied that it felt like that possibly reinforces this notion that "good" work looks a certain way. I feel like this binary of "good" versus "bad" doesn't allow for a more nuanced interpretation of what the study is doing. The reality is it could lead to both good and bad outcomes, right?
>
> Sam: That makes sense. Binary thinking might actually inhibit conversations about how research can have multiple contradictory forms of impact. Work being critical doesn't preclude it from being elitist or guarantee that it has a positive impact on the communities we serve. Work that helps us accumulate accolades and resources doesn't always center our responsibility

to our communities. Bodies of work that center the voices of one
exploited community can reinforce problems faced by others.

Amy: I agree. I think painting a paradigm, framework, or method as
good also assumes that it is going to lead to certain outcomes when
it is a tool, much like a researcher, that can be used or misused.

In this conversation, we question the ways in which neoliberal logics that
promote hyper-competition and capital accumulation shape research
design and detract scholars' attention from prioritizing responsibility to
communities. As researchers, our work is quickly commodified and its
worth measured through the honors it earns in the academy, such as publications in top-tier journals, accrued recognition and awards, and its ability
to generate funding.

What is the impact you hope to see? With whom do you want to experience these outcomes? What are the implications of the research for your
communities, the Indigenous land you inhabit, and the waterways that
surround it? Asking and answering these questions in the research design
process might allow you to better clarify the many intended and unintended
consequences of your work. Doing so might mean that you engage in a continuous struggle with academia's deeply embedded assumptions about what
constitutes impact. It might mean refusing taken-for-granted but unneces-
sary assumptions that impact is about capital accumulation, individual fame
and accolades, and recognition. It might mean working to understand how
your collective communities define desirable impact and prioritizing those
in the design of your work.

Centering Relationships to Cultivate Solidarity in and Through Research

The research process might also be viewed as a strategic tool to foster
relationships that ultimately cultivate solidarity among researchers
and participants. Relationships are not just a tool to execute scholarly
inquiry. They are fundamental to the community and collective struggle
that neoliberalism seeks to erase. As such, the deepening of humanized
relationships that form the tapestry of community can serve as an act of
refusal. Thus, it is important to consider how the research process you
design will (re)shape your relationships with those around you.

Amy: I have increasingly been noticing the competitiveness of the academy, and it makes the work much less enjoyable. From people
being scared to share their work with each other to all of the self-
promotion on social media, it sucks that people have to be so

worried about these things. It makes it hard to foster authentic community.

Sam: I can see how that's frustrating, but I think there are ways we can begin to refuse that hyper-competitiveness. I recently wrote a collaborative piece in which we responded to critiques of scholarship from our community. In writing the piece, we contemplated how hyper-competitive norms might have fueled the critique, how it might shape our desires to respond to it, and how we might minimize the adverse impact of our response on solidarities in the scholarly community. Talking through our internalized competitiveness gave us an opportunity to think about the larger dynamics in the field, and I think it gave the emerging scholars on the piece an opportunity to process what a more caring and collectivist scholarly community could look like.

Amy: True! I have been in spaces where I am able to have those kinds of discussions too, but they don't seem to be very common. I guess the question is, how do we normalize those kinds of conversations?

Settler neoliberal logics fuel individualistic hyper-competition (Grande, 2018), often pitting people against each other and undermining their very capacity to change a system that thrives off of violence moving in any direction (Museus, 2020). Research designs that ignore the role of relationships with communities and the environment are more likely to provide an opening for individualistic hyper-competitive rationalities to seep into the process. Conversely, research designs that intentionally and intimately account for the role of relationships open up possibilities to collectively refuse individualism and foster solidarity.

You can design research in a way that promotes a refusal of individualistic hyper-competition and aims to foster stronger solidarities among scholars advocating for marginalized communities. How can you construct the research process so that a central outcome is to deepen your relationships with those around you, the generations who came before and will come after you within your communities, and your environment?

Concluding Thoughts

Being embedded in a system and part of it means living in a paradox. Research both reinforces existing systems and has the potential to serve as a site of refusal. The task then is to maximize the capacity of scholarly efforts to undermine structures of oppression, minimize the damage from them, and generate space for other possibilities that center marginalized values so that they permeate and drive the execution of scholarly inquiry.

Through this discussion, we seek to raise questions about what such processes might look like and leave you with a few of them to ponder as you move forward with your work. If you view research as an opportunity to engage in transformative reflexivity, what would that look, sound, and feel like? To what communities must you be responsible, and how will you balance those obligations throughout the research process? If you are designing research to advance decolonization and justice goals, how will you intentionally consider the many potential intersections between the research process and the communities with which you advocate?

The answers to these questions are not simple and may not be uniform across contexts, communities, or people. And yet, asking them and centering their implications in the design of our research might free us just a bit more from the constraints of academic conventions and allow us to unlock the full potential power of scholarly research.

References

Ambo, T. (2018). Caregiving as refusal in the academy. *International Journal of Qualitative Studies in Education, 31*(3), 215–222. https://doi.org/10.1080/09518398.2017.1401148

Brown, W. (2006). American nightmare: Neoliberalism, neoconservatism, and de-democratization. *Political Theory, 34*(6), 690–714. http://www.jstor.org/stable/20452506

Chandler, K. L. (2018). I ulu no ka lālā i ke kumu, the branches grow because of the trunk: Ancestral knowledge as refusal. *International Journal of Qualitative Studies in Education, 31*(3), 177–187. https://doi.org/10.1080/09518398.2017.1401146

England, K. V. (1994). Getting personal: Reflexivity, positionality, and feminist research. *The Professional Geographer, 46*(1), 80–89. https://doi.org/10.1111/j.0033-0124.1994.00080.x

Gildersleeve, R. E. (2017). The neoliberal academy of the anthropocene and the retaliation of the lazy academic. *Cultural Studies ↔ Critical Methodologies, 17*(3), 286–293. https://doi.org/10.1177/1532708616669522

Glenn, E. N. (2015). Settler colonialism as structure: A framework for comparative studies of U.S. race and gender formation. *Sociology of Race and Ethnicity, 1*(1), 52–72. https://doi.org/10.1177/2332649214560440

Gonzales, L. D., & Núñez, A. M. (2014). The ranking regime and the production of knowledge: Implications for academia. *Education Policy Analysis Archives, 22*(31), 1–24. https://doi.org/10.14507/epaa.v22n31.2014

Gramsci, A. (1971). *Selections from the Prison Notebooks.* International Publishers.

Grande, S. (2018). Refusing the university. In E. Tuck & K. W. Yang (Eds.), *Toward what justice* (pp. 47–65). Routledge.

Harney, S., & Moten, F. (2013). *The Undercommons: Fugitive planning & Black study*. Minor Compositions.

hooks, b. (2000). *Feminist theory: From margin to center*. Pluto Press.

la paperson. (2017). *A third university is possible*. University of Minnesota Press.

Lather, P. (1991). *Getting smart: Feminist research and pedagogy with/in the postmodern*. Routledge.

Lloyd, D., & Wolfe, P. (2016). Settler colonial logics and the neoliberal regime. *Settler Colonial Studies, 6*(2), 109–118. https://doi.org/10.1080/2201473X.2015.1035361

Museus, S. D. (2020). Humanizing scholarly resistance: Toward greater solidarity in social justice advocacy within the neoliberal academy. *International Journal of Qualitative Studies in Education, 33*(2), 140–150. https://doi.org/10.1080/09518398.2019.1681544

Museus, S. D., & LePeau, L. (2019). Navigating neoliberal organizational cultures: Implications for higher education leaders advancing social justice agendas. In A. Kezar and J. Posselt (Eds.), *Administration for social justice and equity in higher education: Critical perspectives for leadership and decision making* (pp. 209–224). Routledge.

Simpson, A. (2014). *Mohawk interruptus: Political life across the borders of settler states*. Duke University Press.

Slaughter, S. A., & Rhoades, G. (2004). *Academic capitalism and the new economy: Markets, state, and higher education*. Johns Hopkins University Press.

Wolfe, P. (1999). *Settler colonialism*. Cassell.

2

SURVIVANCE-BASED INQUIRIES IN AND BEYOND THE ACADEMY

Angie Morrill and Leilani Sabzalian

W hen sharing about her contribution to the exhibit We Have Teeth Too, at the Berkeley Art Center, our relative and friend, Natalie Ball wrote,

> It's not enough to be dead, you want us murdered. It's not enough to be murdered, you want us dismembered. It's not enough to be in pieces, you want us stolen. And then forgotten. Now, Berkeley's Phoebe A. Hearst Museum holds our stolen Ancestors as ransom. What more could you want? We need our Bones back.
>
> I speak as a tribal citizen, card or not, I speak as a descendant, I speak as a future Ancestor and I speak as a mom who remembers. (Personal communication, October 12, 2020)

The stark cardboard box filled with bright red linen in the middle of the museum's exhibit, coupled with Natalie Ball's demands and desires, is a brilliant act of survivance to open our chapter (see Figure 2.1). Embedded in her installation are the very features and echoes of survivance we hope inspire researchers as they think carefully and critically about their inquiries: an emphasis on Native presence, relationality, continuity, and futures, a refusal to accept colonial conditions, an ethic of responsibility, and traces of wit and humor ("I'll cover shipping"). Natalie Ball's art speaks back to the ongoing violence that museums inflict on Indigenous peoples, but she is neither defined by, nor a victim of such violence; she is a mother, relative, and ancestor whose art and words express a deep love for her people. Natalie's creative and storied insistence on remembering embody

Figure 2.1. Hey Berkeley's Phoebe Hearst Museum, this is Natalie Ball. Put my Bones in the box. Wrap them in the fabric, children, and women first. And return my Ancestors. I'll cover shipping. By Natalie Ball. Photos used with permission.

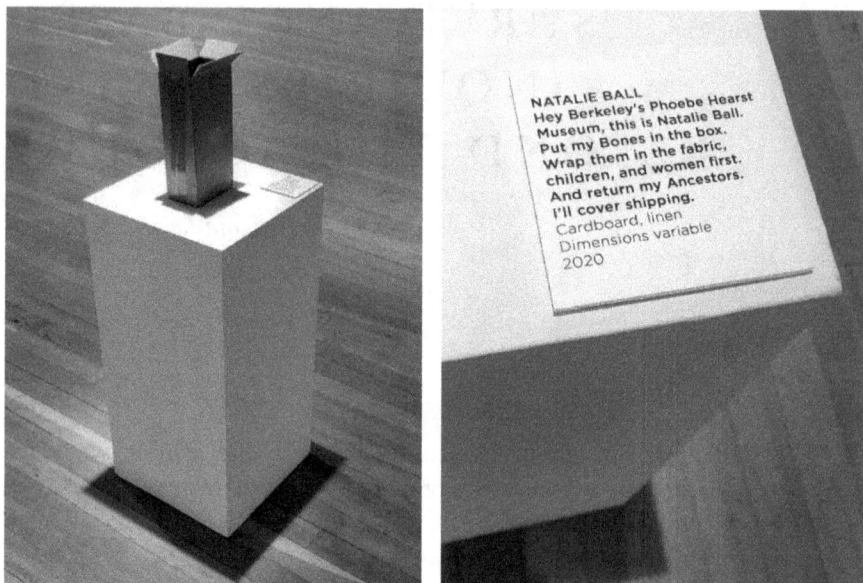

survivance and assert a collective and intergenerational presence and future in a place that has wreaked havoc on her community.

It is fitting that our discussion of survivance follows that of refusal (see chapter 1, this volume), a rich theory and practice that complements our understanding of survivance. As a practice, refusal can be both protective and generative (Simpson, 2007), a way to protect our communities and knowledge systems and sovereignty by refusing to write or tell that which does not benefit our people. Refusal recognizes that our collaborators may contest and refuse the terms of research, and that as researchers we have a responsibility to write in ways that further the integrity, dignity, humanity, and sovereignty of those with whom we research.

Without collapsing the rich and varied meanings and practices of refusal, we recognize an important connection between refusal and survivance. This connection is demonstrated in Natalie Ball's description of her artwork generally, and her contribution to We Have Teeth Too:

> Natalie Ball's current work explores gesture and materiality to create textiles and sculptures as Power Objects. She offers her objects as proposals of refusal to complicate an easily affirmed and consumed narrative and identity, without absolutes . . . to move "Indian" outside of governing

discourses in order to build a visual genealogy that refuses to line up with the many constructed existences of Native Americans. (Ball et al., 2020, paras. 2–3)

Natalie Ball's insistence on refusing prescriptive narratives of Indianness, on refusing simplicity and insisting on the complexity of our lives, a complexity that is central to telling responsible stories of ourselves, our communities, our nations both in the past and today, highlights how survivance and refusal can work together, as partners in decolonial struggles.

For us, survivance has been an embodying of refusal (Simpson, 2007): a practice of refusing to succumb to tragic stories about our lives; a refusal to let colonization be the only story we tell about ourselves, our families, or our communities; a refusal to tell stories about Indigenous lives that are rooted in pathology, victimry, or damage (Tuck, 2009). We also see important connections between survivance and what Unangax̂ scholar Eve Tuck (2009) has referred to as desire-based research. Tuck urges us to refuse research intent on exposing the harm and damage done to our communities, even when we sincerely hope such exposure will benefit us. Research that focuses on documenting "the effects of oppression on our communities," she wrote, can have "the long-term repercussions of *thinking of ourselves as broken*" (p. 409). Instead, Tuck calls us to "craft our research to capture *desire* instead of damage" (p. 416). We propose survivance storytelling as a kin methodology to desire-based research, perhaps a younger sibling or cousin, because her framework has helped us theorize our own.

Survivance

White Earth scholar Gerald Vizenor (2008) coined the term survivance, a semantic combination of survival and resistance, to describe Native peoples' "active resistance and repudiation of dominance" (p. 11); yet survivance exceeds either the term *survival* or *resistance*. Survivance is "more than the potentially dangerous, precipitous act of (metaphorically) hanging on by the skin of your teeth, i.e., surviving, and more than the fixed state implied by the (also metaphorical) digging in of your heels, i.e., resisting" (Watanabe, 2014, p. 157). Taken in this manner, survivance describes "Indigenous creative approaches to life beyond genocide, beyond the bareness of survival" (Morrill, 2017, p. 15).

Key to understanding survivance is the emphasis on Native "*presence over absence, nihility, and victimry*" (Vizenor, 2008, p. 15, emphasis added). As Indigenous peoples, our experiences are diverse and complex, and yet these dimensions of Indigenous life are often ignored or erased in academic and literary representations. Presence is an invitation for us to embody and express the fullness of our lives, a fullness developed over generations of lived and storied experiences. Survivance is "an intergenerational connection to an individual and collective sense of presence and resistance in personal experience . . . and particularly through stories" (Vizenor et al., 2014, p. 108). For us, survivance as an intergenerational and insistent presence amidst colonization has shaped the stories we tell ourselves and each other, the ways we recognize and support one another, and how we imagine and enact our personal and community-based inquiries. Though we will discuss research as a more formal process of inquiry within the academy, we feel it is important to clarify that many of our inquiries involve questions around our own lives, families, and communities. Some of these survivance-based inquiries have found voice in our publications and presentations; others we hold closely, as intimate acts of remembrance, reclamation, reconnection, and recognition (Morrill, 2017; Smith, 2012).

Important to understanding survivance is also Vizenor's (2008) clarification that "survivance is a practice, not an ideology, dissimulation, or a theory" (p. 11). We enact survivance. We story survivance. We dream and imagine and engender survivance. Survivance is also our inheritance. When we feel anxious, insignificant, or inadequate, we can let our legacy of survivance be our source of strength. We can also will survivance into being. As an example, before I (Leilani) had the courage to return to my homelands, I repeatedly told myself a story, a survivance story, written by Koyukon Athabascan poet Mary TallMountain (2005): "I tell you now. You *can* go home again" (p. 13). I told myself I could go home, a telling that eventually enabled me to go home. Though returning to my homelands was an act of survivance, telling the story that made my return possible was also an expression of survivance. Acts of survivance creatively traverse, or perhaps more precisely collapse, the space between the "imaginary" and the "real" (Vizenor, 1999).

Practices of survivance are as diverse as Native people themselves, and these practices surface in both epic and everyday ways (Sabzalian, 2019). It is important to recognize the everydayness of survivance, akin to Hunt and Holmes' (2015) description of everyday decolonization: "While large-scale actions such as rallies, protests and blockades are frequently acknowledged as sites of resistance, the daily actions undertaken by individual Indigenous people, families, and communities often go unacknowledged but are no less vital to decolonial processes" (pp. 157–158). Survivance is expressed in the metastories of Native collective presence and action, Idle No More, Standing Rock, and Mauna Kea. And also, we express survivance in quieter and subtler ways, through looks, gestures, small acts of defiance and reclamation, through reading and writing, through recognition, and more.

Inquiries rooted in survivance might document community-based self-determination: partnerships created between Native nations to establish mutual aid and caretake Elders and families, the creation of survival schools or language programs, the passage of Indigenous studies curriculum mandates; but survivance-based inquiries might also document the creativity and brilliance of a lone Native student navigating a hostile classroom, or a Native student's insistence on wearing regalia to graduation despite their school's "no adornment" policy.

Survivance is embodied by Native feminist theorists whose writings are "practices of reading survivance" (Morrill, 2017, p. 15). As I (Angie) have described elsewhere (Morrill, 2017), survivance informs my "Native feminist reading practice," a methodology of "reading survivance from a place of survivance. . . . A methodology that attends to the transhistorical feminist labor of bearing an Indigenous future into existence out of a genocidal present" (p. 15). In "Time Traveling Dogs (and Other Native Feminist Ways to Defy Dislocations)" (Morrill, 2017), I wrote about a painting by my mother. It was a picture of her and her sisters in the lost city of Vanport, before a flood forced the relocation of the people living there. I read this painting, alongside my mother's star quilts and photo albums of pictures of reservation days, as Native feminist texts. I knew "these quilts, paintings and photographs to be also already reading and writing survivance" (p. 15). As "Native feminist reading and writing practices," they helped me "articulate a methodology . . . to engage the desires, the knowledges, and the futurities in cultural productions by Native women even when these same women are overdetermined within settler produced representations" (p. 15).

Recognizing my mother's paintings and quilts as practices of survivance, recognizing my own reading of them as survivance within a Native feminist legacy of survivance—a "shared ontological project of bearing the future out of a genocidal present" (p. 15)—are ways that I have engaged in survivance-based inquiries. Self-recognition shifts the audience, authority, and approval of my scholarship away from its dominant location (academic institutions or peer reviewers), and instead toward other Native feminists, "Native women and others working actively against settler colonialism and heteropatriarchy and toward decolonization, recognition, and revitalization of Native women and communities" (p. 15). My goal is not recognition from the academy, but self-recognition, and "recognition of and by this community" (p. 15) of Native feminists are critical aspects of my practice.

This future-oriented practice of "reading survivance from a place of survivance" has been an important way of thinking with my (Angie) mother's quilts and paintings, but this practice can be applied in a variety of contexts. I (Leilani) have taken up this practice within the field of Indigenous education, specifically through a methodology of survivance storytelling. As a practice and a commitment, I have looked for the everyday ways Native youth, families, and educators have creatively confronted colonial dynamics and asserted their presence in a public school district that ignores, erases, or demeans them. At times, expressions of survivance were highly visible, such as the communal self-determination of Indigenous families and educators reclaiming space in a district that kept erasing us. The Native youth center we built to create space for our needs and aspirations, for example, was a momentous practice of survivance. But survivance also surfaced in subtler, everyday ways: Native youth contesting colonizing curriculum and asserting their own knowledge; Native youth expressing pride in their identities; or Native youth taking up projects, on their own time outside of class, to learn about ideas and issues that are important to them. As a methodology, survivance storytelling is designed to "reflect back the courage, commitment, and continuity of Native students, educators, and community members" (Sabzalian, 2019, p. 4). Survivance stories recognize Native youth and educators' brilliance as they navigate, defy, and create space for themselves and each other within the colonial terrain of public education. With Native readers in mind, my hope is that recognizing and reflecting back this brilliance—"I see you. I see what you are up against. I also recognize your power" (Sabzalian, 2019, p. xvii)—will encourage self-recognition. Survivance storytelling is a desire-based project designed to recognize, reflect, and engender survivance.

These descriptions of survivance—as presence, as practice, as recognition—lay the groundwork for several stories that we hope reflect and nurture Native survivance. Survivance "is deliberately open . . . with meaning that changes within different context" (Morrill, 2017, p. 15). Survivance is Native feminist reading and writing. Survivance is a commitment to engendering creativity and education and life amidst genocide. Survivance is walking into a museum that stole your ancestors' bones and demanding their return. Before discussing how survivance might inform inquiry, we offer several survivance stories of our own lives and work together.

Survivance Stories

Ts' its' tsi' nako, Thought-Woman, is sitting in her room

and what ever she thinks about appears.

She thought of her sisters,

Nau' ts' ity' i and I' tcs' i,

and together they created the Universe

this world

and the four worlds below.

Thought-Woman, the spider,

named things and

as she named them

they appeared.

She is sitting in her room

thinking of a story now

I'm telling you the story

she is thinking.

—Silko (1977, p. 1)

In *Ceremony,* Silko reminds us what Vizenor (2008) has shared elsewhere: "Native stories are the sources of survivance" (p. 11). To address one of the core questions of this book—how can the practice of research bring us closer to the peoples, places, more than human beings, histories, presents, and futures in which we are embedded and connected to?—we thought it best to tell a few stories.

Survivance Story 1: Survivance and Recognition Can Sustain Us

I am working with my friend and colleague Leilani Sabzalian; we are both Native women, we both work in the field of education. Leilani is a professor in the College of Education at the University of Oregon; she is also co-director of the Sapsik'ʷałá teaching program. I am the chair of the Tribal Advisory Council of the Sapsik'ʷałá program and director of the Title VI Indian Education program, and while Leilani and I were both finishing our dissertations, we worked for the University of Oregon supporting and recruiting Native students. Our story is a story of survivance. When I met Leilani I didn't think she would finish her dissertation; she was working full-time and parenting two small children. I didn't know her. I didn't know she would write her dissertation at the soccer field, that she would apply for and be awarded a prestigious grant to help her finish writing. She not only finished her dissertation, she won an award for it, and then quickly turned it into a book, which also won awards. You don't have to know that Leilani is cringing as I explain these facts, but she is. She also spent time in my office, and as we collaborated in our jobs, we also discussed Native studies, Native feminist methodologies, and different scholars and approaches. This chapter was born then, as we discussed writing together. The fact is, we were practicing survivance through recognition of our roles as Native women, parents, and scholars; through refusal to be limited to only our work; through forging a relationship that would support each other as we navigated difficult terrain. Seven years later we have different roles, but we continue to invest in a relationship that is reciprocal and sustains us. We make each other laugh. We respect each other's work and share it. We continue to recognize each other as scholars, as Native women, and as family.

Survivance is a methodology that stretches and never breaks, that makes room for more, that recognizes the difficult journey that got you here. Survivance includes our ancestors, our ghost stories and hauntings, our children and decolonized futures not yet here. Survivance makes a promise. Survivance is not one thing; it is such an important and useful concept because of its elasticity, its blurred edges and refusal to be defined definitively. It is me remembering my Native professor and mentor telling me that he cries in his office when he is working, because so many of our stories, so much of our research, touches so much damage and violence. It is another friend and mentor asking me 10 years into attempting to finish my dissertation if I would be her writing partner; she would send me daily texts updating me on the progress on her book and I would do the same. Survivance is that kindness that helped me finish when I thought I could not. It is strength and love; it is fierce kindness and a belief in our people, our culture, and our futures.

Survivance Story 2: Survivance and Recognition Are Abundant

Our friendship began when Angie was the coordinator of Native Recruitment and I was the Native retention specialist and academic advisor on campus. We were both mothers and students, and now, we used to joke, we were professional NDN ladies. We were grateful for these jobs that offered us salaries to support Native students. We knew that universities often support the titles of these positions, but not necessarily the responsibilities and commitments that come with them. Regardless, we were thrilled and worked tirelessly to create space on campus for Native students, and through that work, space for ourselves. We demanded the institution take seriously our concerns and priorities, even though we were often treated as tokens. We wiggled our way into important meetings to ask hard questions about recruitment, data collection and reporting, and student services. We did our best to let Native students know that they belonged, that they deserved to be on this campus, that their presence was valued. We also held space for and supported one another in an institution that wanted us to look out for ourselves. We can see now that we approached this work as survivance work.

One example of our survivance-based work was an award ceremony we created to honor Indigenous students, staff, and community members. Rather than competitive, achievement-based awards, we wondered how we might recognize all the good work being done by and for Native people on campus. We wanted to create an award process that wasn't hierarchical, but relational and rooted in recognition and reciprocity. We wanted to create a space for our Native community on campus to see and value and recognize one another. We wanted to counter the academy's value of scarcity with abundance.

Together we dreamed up an award process rooted in the concepts of survivance and recognition. Our community nominated and presented awards to one another and told stories of why we valued one another. We recognized students who demonstrated leadership in their classes, as well as those who managed to finish that incomplete that had been hanging over their heads. We recognized Elders and community members who brought food to potluck each week and showed up to encourage students. We recognized people who created highly visible programs as well as those who worked tirelessly behind the scenes. We shared food and laughter and tears. We created space to see and value one another. The awards are still a part of campus, now named The PRIDE Awards: Proudly Recognizing Indigenous Devotion to Education. Our dear friend Stephanie Tabibian also added a new element, gifting honorees with art created by Indigenous students or alumni. The gifted art by students varied each year. Here we are sharing one piece (Figure 2.2), Strong Stalk by Diné artist Jacinthia Stanley, which exemplifies survivance.

Universities are often sites of dispossession, erasure, and harm for Native students, and because of this, many of the students we worked with spent a great deal of time contesting the colonialism they experience in the university and engaging in survivance work to create space for themselves, for each other, and for those who will follow; but this work can also be depleting and distract us from nurturing our own power. The award Stanley created, Strong Stalk, reminded students that our insistence on knowing who we are and where we come from is an inherent critique of settler colonialism. Stanley reminded students that our lands, our lifeways, and our ancestors are always with us, always here for us. From our work with some of the students, we knew they didn't feel confident or connected to who they were or where they came from, but survivance is generous and generative. Stanley shared her knowledge and teachings, and while some of the students gifted the piece understood the line "You are a corn stalk, a strong stalk" to be true, others

Figure 2.2. Strong Stalk by Jacinthia "Jay" Stanley (Diné).

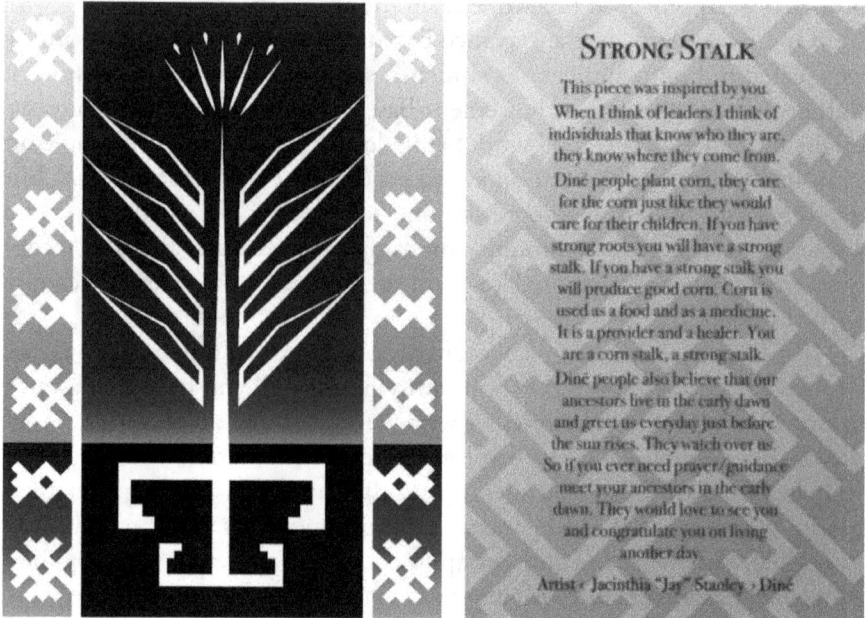

needed to hear it, maybe even needed to repeat it, for it to be so. Survivance and recognition are abundant and can be catalysts for remembering and regenerating our power as Indigenous peoples.

Survivance Story 3: Survivance and Recognition Can Help Us Reclaim and Reconnect

Recognition is not just a feel-good process, though it can make us feel good. Recognition can restore and regenerate. Recognition can heal, and in my case, recognition helped me re-member my way back into my relations.

I was older when I reconnected with my village in Alaska. As an adoptee, my connection to kin and community was disrupted. It took decades to find my family, to reach out to relatives who might consider hosting a relative two generations removed from village life, to return to my homelands. It took countless hours combing through adoption records, court cases, and other archives. It also took determination and courage, a willingness to be vulnerable, a willingness to be rejected. Though an expression of survivance, I believe my desire and willingness to return to my homelands was, in fact, driven by the very concept.

As a Native adoptee, I've navigated multiple dimensions of dispossession and belonging; like other adoptees, I've navigated questions about my "real" family, while also navigating discourses of authenticity and whether I was "really" Indigenous if I was raised by a White family. At times, my anxieties have almost swallowed me, almost erased me. But Native feminist practices of survivance and recognition—many of them taught to me by my dear friend Angie—have shown me that we are more than our dispossession stories. Survivance has taught me that colonialism has created the conditions of my dispossession from my home and homelands, or my anxieties about belonging, and that teaching—that there are structures that have tried to harm me, and that I am still here in spite of them—has been powerful. Survivance is feeling seen by Angie, a bone-deep recognition that let me know I am enough. Survivance is also the practice of speaking our strength into being. Mary TallMountain (2005) told me, "You *can* go home again" (p. 13), and I told myself that survivance story until I believed it could be true, until I made it true. And this small survivance story has opened up a very different future for my children than I had.

Survivance is a reminder that we can refuse to pathologize ourselves, that we can remember, reclaim, and reconnect, and that our presence within our network of relations is our rightful inheritance.

*   *   *   *

Through these three stories, we described how our university-based student services work together, which we viewed as survivance work. These survivance stories are inquiries: How can we continue to see one another in a place so adamant on devaluing us? How can we create space for ourselves, our students, our communities, in a place built on Indigenous erasure and dispossession? How can we subvert university aims and divert university resources to serve our Indigenous aspirations? How can we feel good about ourselves and find our way home? How can we recognize the ways survivance necessarily moves us beyond "formal" academic research? We hope these stories describing our practices of recognition, of space-making, of crafty self-determination, are helpful as you imagine and enact your own survivance-based inquiries.

Considerations for Survivance-Based Inquiries

We were invited to think through how survivance influences "how we pause and come to our study designs, as we warp our research, as qualitative researchers" and how survivance strengthens our relationality. For us, survivance has been a way of recognizing one another, a practice of seeing, supporting, and affirming our lives and our work as Native feminists in a colonizing institution. As Angie shared, this chapter was born years ago, as we each worked to create space for ourselves and other Native students at a university campus. We were practicing survivance, a practice of recognition that engendered survivance.

Survivance has also shaped how we have conducted our formal academic inquiries. For me (Angie), survivance was a practice of recognizing that our academic inquiries could be personal, an affirmation I learned through reading Dian Million's (2013) felt theory. Million's writing about the affect and emotion in Native women's narratives, which "simultaneously designate them as incomprehensible in the white academy," created space for me "to draw on my ancestors, their lives, their stories, and their refusals" (Morrill, 2017, p. 15). I had been "warned by academic mentors, that I was going to have to be very careful if I wanted to present family pictures, family stories, quilts, and artwork as scholarship" (p. 16), but Million's commitment to reading Native women's lives through a Native feminist lens created space for my own practice and commitment of reading Native women's survivance from a lens of survivance. I was able to engage in felt theory scholarship about "locating home, surviving dispossession, claiming space, and listening to ghosts" and recognize these as "shared Indigenous projects, rather than strictly academic ones" (p. 16). I saw myself as part of a "transhistorical community of readers and writers" (p. 15), a network of Native women "who recognize—a felt knowledge of what you do that impacts what I do" (p. 16).

Survivance is an intergenerational practice, and with respect to inquiry, a practice of asking questions that make space for ourselves, our families, and for others who follow, a practice of asserting our presence, our priorities, our aspirations. Survivance is Million writing to Angie. Survivance is Angie writing to me (Leilani), and other Native feminist scholars wanting to write in life-affirming ways. Survivance is a way to create space for our presence, including the complexities and contradictions of our lives. Survivance is a practice of recognition and space-making.

In designing inquiries, we offer that survivance is a practice of asking questions that affirm and recognize and engender survivance. These can be personal questions, for the personal work we do as Native researchers is also important intergenerational work. These questions can also be commitments, a willingness to look for the spaces we/other Native peoples create for ourselves, for our communities, for our languages and lifeways. Our Yakama colleague Michelle Jacob's scholarship offers a beautiful model of survivance-based inquiry, a way of reading and writing the world that both reflects and reproduces survivance. In her book *Yakama Rising: Indigenous Cultural Revitalization, Activism, and Healing*, Jacob (2013) documents various members of her community engaging in cultural revitalization projects, including the Wapato Indian Dance Club, Ichishkíin language activism, and educational workshops designed to sustain traditional Yakama foodways. Survivance takes many forms in this book: stories of Native youth asserting their presence and embodying decolonizing praxis amid a state anniversary celebration; stories of a small group of language activists who "helped to subvert the colonial assimilationist agenda designed to eliminate our language" (p. 52); stories of intergenerational grassroots food activism designed to foster Native youth and communities' physical, cultural, and spiritual connections to traditional foods.

Jacob's theory of Yakama decolonizing praxis, which involves "(1) understanding indigenous bodies as sites of critical pedagogy, (2) centering social justice praxis to build a moral community, and (3) utilizing grassroots indigenous resistance as a mechanism to dismantle colonial logics" (p. 16) reflects the iterative nature of survivance-based methodologies. Her inquiry sought to reflect the survivance in her community, and in so doing informed her understanding of Yakama decolonizing praxis. This survivance-based inquiry created space for Yakama presence and survivance. Survivance-based inquiries engender survivance.

Storytelling is such an important vehicle for survivance. As Vizenor (1999) shares, language did the capturing, and so language can also be liberating. Colonization has involved discursive tropes that entrap us in a practice of seeing Indians, of becoming Indians. But survivance combats "literary annihilation" (p. 8) with Native presence. Survivance stories not only contest the "literature of dominance" by subverting and refusing simulations of Indianness, but survivance stories create space for our complex presences. Survivance stories are diverse in form and content: sometimes they tease, sometimes they attack, sometimes they speak of something else altogether. Survivance stories deflate worn-out ideas that bring us down, or refashion words and language to make them potent. Survivance stories try to imagine something different.

Survivance as Our Shared Legacy

This chapter sought to describe how survivance can guide (but not prescribe) approaches to inquiry (only some of which take place in the academy). Survivance-based inquiries defy colonialism but aren't defined by it. And because acts and stories of survivance are as diverse as Native peoples, survivance-based inquiries will differ in form, in content, in intent. Survivance is reclaiming our bones, recognizing the genius in our quilts and our paintings, memorizing poems until they become our lives, writing the world that we want to live in. Survivance-based inquiries are those questions and practices and writings that reflect and nurture Native survivance.

By documenting stories that connected us to one another, stories that held us up, stories that took us home, stories that honored or unleashed our creativity, stories that recognize the beauty and brilliance of Native youth and families, we offer survivance as a practice of defiance and reclamation that can meaningfully shape inquiries, a practice that can heal and sustain us, a method that can help us remember, restore, and reconnect. As a practice, we hope survivance can connect Indigenous researchers to the legacy of courage, creativity, intelligence, determination, and artfulness that our people have embodied since Time Immemorial.

References

Ball, N., Craig, J. A., Robbins, M., & Roy, A. (2020). *We have teeth too.* Berkeley Art Center. https://www.berkeleyartcenter.org/we-have-teeth-too-virtual-exhibition

Hunt, S., & Holmes, C. (2015). Everyday decolonization: Living a decolonizing queer politics, *Journal of Lesbian Studies, 19*(2), 154–172. https://doi.org/10.1080/10894160.2015.970975

Jacob, M. (2013). *Yakama rising: Indigenous cultural revitalization, activism, and healing.* University of Arizona Press.

Million, D. (2013). *Therapeutic nations: Healing in an age of indigenous human rights.* University of Arizona Press.

Morrill, A. (2017). Time traveling dogs (and other Native feminist ways to defy dislocations). *Cultural Studies ↔ Critical Methodologies, 17*(1), 14–20. https://doi.org/10.1177/1532708616640564

Sabzalian, L. (2019). *Indigenous children's survivance in public schools.* Routledge.

Silko, L. M. (1977). *Ceremony.* Penguin Books.

Simpson, A. (2007). On ethnographic refusal: Indigeneity, "voice," and colonial citizenship. *Junctures,* (9), 67–80.

Smith, L. T. (2012). *Decolonizing methodologies: Research and indigenous peoples* (2nd ed.). Zed Books.

TallMountain, M. (2005). You *can* go home again: A sequence. In B. Swanson & A. Krupat (Eds.), *I tell you now: Autobiographical essays by Native American writers* (pp. 1–13). University of Nebraska Press.

Tuck, E. (2009). Suspending damage: A letter to communities. *Harvard Educational Review, 79*(3), 409–428. https://doi.org/10.17763/haer.79.3.n0016675661t3n15

Vizenor, G. R. (1999). *Manifest manners: Narratives on post-Indian survivance.* University of Nebraska Press.

Vizenor, G. R. (Ed.). (2008). *Survivance: Narratives of Native presence.* University of Nebraska Press.

Vizenor, G., Tuck, E., & Yang, K. W. (2014). Resistance in the blood. In E. Tuck & K. W. Yang (Eds.), *Youth resistance research and theories of change* (pp. 107–117). Routledge.

Watanabe, S. (2014). Critical storying: Power through survivance and rhetorical sovereignty. In J. Flores Carmona & K. V. Luschen (Eds.), *Crafting critical stories: Toward pedagogies and methodologies of collaboration, inclusion and voice* (pp. 153–170). Peter Lang.

3

"IF YOU CAN'T GO TO BELLA NOCHE'S . . ."

On the Onto-Epistemological Possibilities for Qualitative Researchers

Reginald Blockett, Leonard D. Taylor Jr., and Steve D. Mobley Jr.

Toni Cade Bambara's 1980 book *The Salt Eaters* raised and answered questions about the ongoing material and symbolic struggle on Black people, especially Black women, in society. Invoking agency and leveraging indifference, Bambara (1980) invites oppressed readers to (re)consider what it means to be well, as well as our role in our own wellness. Specifically, Bambara (1980) invites a sensitivity to, a sensibility of, and dominance over the miseries we are made to experience, as a consequence of our various social and political locations. The invitations and the circumstances that motivate them are especially relevant to Black queer communities broadly, and in the academy specifically.

The various oppressions and complexities that Black queer faculty and students face and navigate are well documented (Alexander, 2005; Blockett, 2017; Means et al., 2017; Mobley & Johnson, 2019). While explicating these oppressions and complexities is important, it is equally important to resist tragically queer narratives that cast Black queer people as abhorrent, bereft of joy, thriving, and possibility (Mobley et al., 2019, 2020; Nunokawa, 1991). Here, Bambara's (1980) invitations to agency—to make sense of and make a change in our relationship with suffering—manifest in our creation of and engagement with the kinship community, which we affectionately refer to as "Bella Noche's," or Bella's for short. In *The Salt Eaters*, Mrs. Sophie Heywood counseled, "[You] have to be whole to see whole" (Bambara, 1980, p. 92), addressing Obie and other activists in the novel who feel the liberation movement slipping and sifting through their grasp. Relatedly, these invitations demand reflection about wholeness and its necessity. For us, this question provided divine insight into the utility and impact of our kinship community on our work as scholars and qualitative researchers. As much as we each sought and seek to do research that changes/improves the material conditions of others toward wellness and wholeness, we had to all be and maintain the well and whole versions of ourselves in the academy. Bella Noche's became the space in which we could do just that.

For us, this question raised others: What do you have to know/experience of community to be able to cultivate community in research relationships? Can you be "in community" with participants/coresearchers if you are not in community with them beyond the research project? Ultimately, our experiences in Bella's have and continue to inform our work and sensibilities as qualitative researchers. Coming to know, understand, and experience community in increasingly intimate/personal ways during research processes not only underscores its sanctity but challenges us to cocreate similar sanctuaries in the communities that form as a part of our research.

Qualitative inquiry is, at its core, relational, and at its best, it ought to be humanizing. To achieve this, qualitative researchers have to understand and desire humanity. Because we intended and constructed Bella's to be a more humanizing space, it made sense that our time and experiences in Bella's informed our understanding of humanity and thus qualitative research. In this chapter, as we seek to engage in research practices that are done with and not on our people (Mobley, 2017), we reflect on how we employ kinship and community to cull and engage our own understandings of and desire for humanity, relation, and healing and flesh those understandings out in our research with/in community of others. Specifically, we highlight how our onto-epistemological kinship space, Bella Noche's, informs our approaches to qualitative research. We also consider how engaging in this onto-epistemological project is a rejoinder to conventional ways of knowing and doing qualitative inquiry.

Reckoning With Onto-Epistemic Violence

For us, Bella Noche's is both sanctuary and refuge from the material and ideological violence we experience in the world and the academy. We were confronted with this violent reality from the onset of our experiences in the academy, as is the case with many Black men on the margins of mainstream gender, sexual, and emotional performance (Alexander, 2005; Means et al., 2017; Mobley et al., 2020). Before we knew each other, each of us knew the academy. We had already experienced its promises and perils and were confronted with the myriad ways various constructs and contexts shaped our social and material conditions (Boykin, 2005; Cole & Guy-Sheftall, 2003; Mitchell & Means, 2014).

For Leonard and Steve, these realities were brought further into relief during their transitions into faculty life in the United States' South. Considering the historical and contemporary legacy of anti-Black and anti-queer violence in the South, Leonard's and Steve's imagined Black queer faculty futures were steeped in and tempered by threats of violence (Mobley et al., 2020). For Reggie, threats were mounted from Black students in the classroom. Reggie experienced the harsh realities of not being seen as a knower and expert by other Black students. All of these hard realities made us each pause and eventually convene time for Bella's.

Through these transitions, and a dogged commitment to living and being in ways that felt authentic and affirming, Reggie, Leonard, and Steve figured out how to be: existing and resisting in their various contexts. We were confronted with challenges, some of which were expected, but many others that none of them could have prepared for or anticipated, experiences not taught in graduate school. Among the most glaring were the ways our bodies and the identities we constructed were explicitly and implicitly sites and sources of contest (Mobley et al., 2020), and often at the hands of close colleagues who imagined themselves to be more self-aware than they perhaps were. Our bodies and ourselves always seemed up for debate and ripe for revisionist interpretations. Colleagues, students, and sometimes other Black queer men made us into caricatures, in service to their raced and gendered imaginings (Mobley et al., 2020).

Community was the beginning—respite from the enduring challenges we experienced while navigating the academy and episodic relief from the dull, incessant suffering prescribed for Black queer men in the academy specifically, and society broadly. Amidst, despite, and in response to these challenges, we engaged in what many describe as queer world-making (Blockett, 2017, 2018). We convened, cackled, and conjured realities that suited our needs, academically, socially, and spiritually. We were called and called each other to joy—a joy beyond relief. This joy manifested explicitly through a summer communing in New Orleans.

Kinship and Black Queer World-Making

We had been convening via phone and iMessage for months before we got the idea to come together in person. It's not uncommon for Black faculty to get together for writing retreats, so it was not the first time we thought about convening. However, this was certainly the first time the community that we had cultivated in the virtual/digital space was to be constructed in the flesh—that is, the real material world. We had all talked and written about our experiences as Black faculty, navigating the academy and the daunting pressure to conform. Our trip to New Orleans, which occurred during Juneteenth, was replete with Black queer expression. New Orleans and our shared space became a world where we could enjoy the relief of unmitigated expression and existence. We wrote a lot, ate too much, drank just enough, and danced as much as we could. As James Baldwin (2013) expressed in *The Fire Next Time*, as he reminisced on Black joy, "We had the liquor, we had the chicken, the music, and each other, and had no need to pretend to be what we were not" (p. 41). For us who shared space, Bella's was a divine opportunity to flesh—to be, in ways that are not always possible or safe. That space to flesh became a world, wherein each of us was committed to being our authentic, vulnerable, and expressive selves authentically in our unabashed Black queerness. We used each other and our community to remind us of who we were.

In those moments, we realized Bella Noche's is corporeal, a space to and of flesh, in resistance to our incessant erasure and misrepresentation in academic and nonacademic spaces (Okello, 2020). Representation is often an intimate and political journey for Black queer and trans people in the academy (Lewis, 2011; Means et al., 2017; Mobley et al., 2020; Stewart, 2016). Along this journey, as many Black people find themselves doing, we are constantly emerging from an academy that has little regard for uncontrolled Blackness (Harris & Njoku, 2017). Similarly, Black queer and trans people, even within Black communities, are having to resist being ushered into normativity (Allen, 2009). Beyond or perhaps in service to our emergence, we had to clear space and make the space to flesh, in an unapologetic and untainted embodiment of our Black queer faculty selves. Whether in person or virtually, the clearing became and continues to be our world.

Not only was Bella's a product of our Black queer world-making, but it also invited us to share and convene our existing worlds, in acts of Black queer world-merging. During our next convening in Detroit, Bella's personal worlds coalesced as we engaged with and were hosted by Reggie and his family. Engaging Reggie and being welcomed by his family required trust. Will Steve and Leonard be welcomed in ways that reflect the safety that we know Reggie to feel in his Black queer identity? Will Leonard and Steve see and engage Reggie's family with love and respect? We were pushed (or invited) to consider each other's existing worlds, to share them with each other, to learn and respect them, and to be held and affirmed by them.

After nearly a year since the last convening of Bella's in Detroit at the end of 2019, we reunited for an intimate extended stay at Leonard's new home in Auburn. On our second night together, Reggie posed a question to the group while communing over dinner: If you had to describe Bella's in just a few words, what comes to mind? This question evoked an array of responses ranging from love, friendship, and freedom to authenticity, fun, and pleasure. As we pondered this question, we found ourselves defining what Bella's is by naming what Bella's does. By that we mean that Leonard so eloquently explained what happens when Bella's is fleshed and actualized during our convenings:

> Leonard: We sitting here eating this good-ass food (sounds of fried shrimp crunching in Steve's mouth) . . . drinking these good-ass drinks. Having this good-ass discussion.
>
> Reggie: (Chewing) And I don't know that I've eaten this good in . . . I don't know when.
>
> Steve: Hunnie! (laughing)
>
> Leonard: So, let's talk about that hunnie. Cause one of the things we do unintentionally is we plan for meals (bites into fried shrimp). You know what I'm saying, and when you think about that from a Black perspective, a Black ancestral perspective, the importance of food and meals. And we don't be like "we have to eat this at Bella's because we MUST fill our souls"; it's just this inherent feeling of "ohh bitch we gon' eat good," because that's a part of being in community. When we think about this idea of fleshing, Bella's is the material component of community. I'm feeding my spirit, I'm feeding my soul, I'm feeding my body; I'm pleasing my spirit, I'm pleasing my soul, I'm pleasing my body.

Bella's is where we make our world, in spite of the systemic forces that actively attempt to negate our places in the academy and the broader societal context. What Leonard articulates in his comment is that Bella's is a space of actuality, one where thinking adjoins sensing and clears and changes the space(s) in the process. It is at Bella's that we feed one another, both literally and figuratively. By showing up as our authentic selves and expecting that we each live our best lives, we defy/transcend expectations/aspirations for legibility. And as we stated in a recent podcast (see Snipes, 2020), we are not striving to be legible to a nonqueer, non-Black gaze. In other words, Bella's transcends the White cisgender heteronormative gaze, which often marks Black queers as tragic or invisible. Here, we share how we cultivate kinship in Bella's not in response to, but despite how we are read.

Kinship is a central formation to Black queer life worlds (Green, 2019; Shange, 2019). The practice of comrades laboring to create and sustain community is common among Black queer communities. Bella's is the product of what happens when we flesh Black queer space. It is a manifestation when Black Queer folks take a sincere onus in actively seeking pleasure and lovingly laboring to create and sustain a sacred Black queer refuge. Bailey (2013) described Black queer space as "the place-making practices that Black LGBT people undertake to affirm and support their non-normative sexual identities, embodiments, and community values and practices" (p. 146).

For us, kinship describes the social, cultural, and political camaraderie produced when we flesh our community space. Carol Stack (1975) reminds us in her important ethnography, *All Our Kin*, "Who is socially recognized as kin depends largely upon the cultural interpretation" (p. 46). Kinship networks have long been a critical component of survival within Black queer life (Hawkeswood, 1996). In ballroom culture, for example, LGBTQ communities of color rely on family ties. Bailey (2013) explained:

> Rather, gay families and queer kin are often established out of necessity and on their own terms . . . kinship among Black LGBTQ communities makes clear that heterosexuality is not the sine qua non of family. Instead, family is about and based on the kin labor that members choose to undertake. (pp. 94–95)

Kin labor rests at the crux of what we do to make Bella's the loving and liberated space that it is. Each of us must work in this space to sustain one another. The product of our labor of love is Bella's, where the confluence of sensual, emotional, and intellectual work comes to life. In "Chatting Back an Epidemic: Caribbean Gay Men, HIV/AIDS, and the Uses of Erotic Subjectivity," Gill (2012) purported that Caribbean gay men engage in erotic subjectivity to make sense of their political, sensual, and spiritual journeys as they survive the HIV/AIDS pandemic. Expanding the erotic theorizing done by Audre Lorde, Gill explained:

> Erotic subjectivity is at once an interpretive perspective and a mode of consciousness; it is both a way of reading and a way of being in the world. This analytic frame encourages a recognition of the fact that systems of colonial (as well as neocolonial/imperial) domination depends partly on a tripartite strategy of coercion based on a politics of ontological racial difference, a hierarchy of spiritual rectitude, and a Victorian sense of (sexual) respectability—erotic subjugation, as it were. (pp. 279–280)

Gill uses this framework to analyze the space-making practices of Caribbean gay men who use the "Chatroom," a dialogue group sponsored by the Trinidad-based nongovernmental organization Friends for Life (FFL). This "fleshy actual space" (Gill, 2012, p. 278) allows for open discussion amongst participants. The space is necessary for the men in Gill's study, many of whom are living with HIV/AIDS and are in need of community building to survive the violence, both material and discursive, that impedes their livelihood. Spaces like the Chatroom are critical, even if just for weekly check-ins, and have a significant effect on the subject formations of Black gay men in the Caribbean region. Through interconnections of the political, the sensual, and the spiritual engagements of the Chatroom, the use of erotic subjectivity "challenges apolitical, passionless, and secular interpretations of how we come to know what we know about ourselves, each other, and our world" (p. 279). Interventions like the Chatroom, and other dialogic groups, are examples of Black queer space-making that arise as acts of resistance, which Gill describes as the praxis of survival. The Chatroom serves as a figurative sacred space, providing ongoing respite and fellowship. This analysis highlights the usefulness of recognizing an interlinked spiritual–sensual–political (erotic) subjectivity for a grassroots struggle to survive in the midst of the vicious HIV/AIDS pandemic. Moreover, erotic subjectivity is a form of Black queer world-making that describes the affective labor of Bella's.

As colleagues and friends, we often find ourselves writing, working, and existing in a space that invites (or demands) maximum expression. This is illustrative of the ways our kinship is not just outside of or in response to the academy but permeates and transcends the academy. By being our full selves, each of us has found more opportunities to bring all of who we are to our work. This may have been most poignant for Leonard, who, until Bella's, had not made deliberate efforts to intersect his queer identity with(in) his research. Finding space to be, make sense of, and imagine himself beyond the academic gaze, Leonard pursued and achieved new possibilities in his scholarship. On late-night phone calls, full of complaint and imagination, we would curse and lament the uphill battle each of us felt. Steve would regularly and assumingly remind us, "We don't write scared!" Writing scared, for us, was giving in to the normativity that we worked so hard to resist; diluting ourselves or our scholarship to better "fit" into the preexisting landscape of the academy. The social/relational ties that were strengthened through Bella's proved to be both developmental and productive for personal and career well-being. These experiences reflect deeper and more complex implications related to the importance of community, not just for ourselves, but for our work.

Qualitative Inquiry

We have come to see the various ways our engagement with others and communities, especially for the purpose of qualitative inquiry, are shaped by the ways we engage and experience relationships and communities ourselves. The kinship, fugitivity, and futurity that we find in/through Bella's has offered each of us new and refreshed understandings of community. Those new and refreshed understandings have induced us to consider how, if we find so much value and humanity in our experiences within community, we might cultivate similar communal experiences for those we engage through our own research. More specifically, we find ourselves responsible to those with whom we work within our research; their experiences during our time together, their reflections during our time apart, and the impact of the work we generate with them.

Unsettling Research Socialization

A key pivot in scholars' development comes as they reflect on and reconsider what they have been taught to be true. Bella's has shaped our onto-epistemological understandings of what community is, means, and can be. In turn, we feel compelled to bring these understandings to bear on/in the relationships that are foundational to our respective approaches to qualitative inquiry. Bella's became a space we also used to interrogate and reconcile our personal, political, cultural, and historic sensibilities—pause—and collectively reimagine the research process.

Reimagining the research process began as we used each other as mirrors to notice, reflect, and map the ways we have and continue to be socialized as researchers and scholars. Through this critical remembering, we engage with our previous experiences and past selves to interrogate the condition they were born from, and imagine new ones (Patton, 2018). Bella's, as a space for critical remembering, has helped us to resist scholarly normativity and various ways the academy tried to cajole young scholars into fitting into past and passed versions of the academy. Through this resistance, Bella's helps us toward what Crawley (2015) discussed as *an institutional*—striving for buoyancy, nimbleness, agility; being open, nuanced, and rigorous. Rather than succumb to the subtle, incessant, insidious pull toward normalcy of the academy, we construct an otherwise. As Crawley explains:

> To be attentive to otherwise possibilities for our existence, to think otherwise possibilities for modes of inhabitation, for means to perform the love and care of flesh is to live into the ongoing resistance that will have

already begun, a resistance to stilling and stasis, a resistance to severance and violence. (p. 88)

In Bella's we found ourselves pursuing, rather than foreclosing, possible ways of being as Black queer scholars within the academy and world; constructing, rather than accepting, ways of being qualitative researchers; and enjoying, rather than suppressing, ways of being human and sharing in humanity with others. Creating space for an otherwise challenges us to unsettle our prior socialization and imagine more humanizing and communal approaches. As a part of that work, we reflected on the notions of responsibility, permission, and labor.

Responsibility

Bringing personal understandings of and experiences with community to bear on research relationships is paramount, as these sensibilities help to focus less on the various power dynamics that might shape or constrain relations, and more on understanding how others experience the relations that emerged from the research interactions. A question that Leonard often reflects on in research projects with practitioners and administrators is "To what extent do different people in the research relationship feel free and affirmed in their institutional or social identities?" For Leonard, who often works with practitioners and administrators in higher education, he has been challenged to understand the tensions they navigate and the affective impact those tensions have on their work and work experiences. The cultural divide between faculty and administrators that persists in higher education automatically places him in tension with many of the people with whom he engages in his research. Insofar as he seeks to challenge and change these divides, he must also understand his position in them and how he propagates through his faculty role. Acknowledging these tensions and privileges is key so that he might work against them to create/cultivate a different set of relations amongst these actors.

In addition to the power that faculty status affords in the context of the academy, it is important to understand how some shared or similar social identities create ties and community in ways that transcend institutional roles. For example, while being a faculty member might be a barrier to understanding and accessing the experiences of an entry-level practitioner if both the practitioners and researchers identify as Black, other avenues and opportunities for connection emerge. Understanding these and other examples of institutional and social location make clear the ways that research interactions can simultaneously reflect and transcend power asymmetries.

By making space for the ways that interactions with others can reinscribe and resist power asymmetries, Leonard does his best to interrupt and embrace them. In the instances where interruption is possible, he works to dismantle or redistribute stratified power dynamics. This might be accomplished by inviting participants to determine the time and location and platform of research conversations or asking for feedback, insight, and suggestions on which kinds of topics or questions would be better to discuss during research conversations. When an interruption is less feasible, such as interacting with Black women in practitioner roles (where Leonard might be seen to have dominant social and institutional locations), Leonard strives to take ownership of and responsibility for the power afforded to him in these research relationships. Regardless of how well developed and affirming communities and relationships are, researchers must always be responsible for the power they are afforded and to the communities and relationships that emerge as a result of their research.

Permission

"Oh Steve, don't go there," others would warn. "There" is a metaphor that has been placed before Steve many times during his time in the academy. For Steve, the following epithet from Vanessa Williams—the first Black Miss America, spoke greatly to his experience(s) in life and his work in the academy:

> You know with my generation and the elders of our generation people didn't talk about the experiences that haunted them or that were disturbing. . . . They were left unsaid. So, there are a lot of mysteries within African-American society. . . . We don't know a lot of the stories that have happened because of the fact that people don't talk about everything. (Williams & Berlinger, 2014)

Her words illuminated the unapologetically bold manner in which she owned and told her story. Williams felt that her voice should be heard because so many before her had chosen, or were forced, to silence theirs. In this instance, she owned her privileged platform and removed her veneer—a mask that she could have used to conceal and hide behind. She sought to rise above and show what laid beneath a tarnished crown and myriad accolades. Why is it that Black communities choose to keep some stories of our pasts hidden? Williams's story struck a chord with him because she went "there"— willingly and openly engaging in topics and spaces thought to be too taboo or unsavory for public acknowledgment. Communing in intimately Black queer spaces, with Black queer people, Steve found permission to go there and finds joy in the journey.

Like many others, Steve has been warned by colleagues, friends, and even family members about doing the work that he endeavors to do—speaking truth to power about Blackness in a very public manner. "Steve, are you sure you wanna go there?" they ask. These warnings, the questions, at one point caused him anxiety, but he pushed forward toward there in his scholarly inquiry, not only for his people but for his personhood. For Steve, Bella Noche's has been a space where he has experienced and provided love and affirmation to go there by choice. As he went there, Leonard and Reggie would often go there with him—to visit and dwell in scholarly spaces that are both uncomfortable and joyous, spaces that live and breathe in his and all of our work. In considering the aforementioned, Black queer issues have remained untouched by many Black, queer, and Black queer higher education scholars. This is understandable on many fronts due to real and imagined risks and privilege some exercise in avoiding them. Bella's provided a freeing space for us to exist beyond risks, providing others an example and invitation to do the same. In one of the final sentences of her book *Their Eyes Were Watching God*, Hurston (1937) wrote, "You have to go there to know there" (p. 193). All of the work that Steve has wanted to do and yearns to explore free him more each time.

Labor

For Reggie, the labor of kinship building has entered his work intrinsically and inseparably from the research process. Conventional ethnographic research works to maintain boundaries between the researcher and the research subject. Even in this anthropological approach to social science research, culture is intended to be observed rather than co-experienced. I (Reggie) was socialized to these practices when he was studying to be a qualitative researcher. But during my time in queer kinship spaces with other budding qualitative researchers, I learned the value of community in the research process. I saw what barriers are created when camaraderie is not established. The lack of kin labor—that is, the sustaining of family—deteriorates the cultural site under investigation, dislodges "strong objectivity" (Harding, 1995) in the research design, and ultimately ruptures the potential catalytic validity (Lather, 1986).

Through the fleshing, clearing, and world-making we were unknowingly theorizing a way of Black queer being that we also draw from as we continue to edit our approaches to inquiry (Lorde, 1984). The agency we exercise helps us to envision and craft a future that is considerate of but not solely responsible to the past and present versions of the academy. We work to unsettle and interrogate our sensibilities and disentangle ourselves from narrow and unimaginative ways of being and knowing. We dream and imagine, build our capacities for dreaming and imagination, and in this Black queer scholarly safe haven we collectively (re)imagine the academy.

Though these reflections on Bella's as community, kinship, and possibility have bearing on our identities, sensibilities, and approaches to inquiry, there is a certain precarity that comes with naming/describing oneself "in community" with others. Who has the power or authority to make that determination? How does/can such naming suggest and enforce rigidity and resist the fluidity of social relations inherent in social science research? Additionally, regardless of the powered dynamics and affective dimensions of researchers' relationships with participants/communities, researchers need those relationships that might invite the exertion of control and feelings of propriety. These needs, if not monitored, can lead to the abuse researchers have been known to cause. By entering the relational, through Bella's, we are in part disrupting and unsettling (although not destroying completely) the propriety (and arguably, coloniality) involved in research relationships (Patel, 2014).

Within Bella's our fugitivity, humanity, and sensibilities are interwoven, becoming a powerful heuristic through which to hold community, to capture and name the joy and growth that comes from being in community, and to consider the presence or absence of these things when engaged with others in research processes. Doing qualitative research automatically places us in a sociocultural community with others. Understanding of community, more especially the onto-epistemological and material ways we have come to know and experience community, shapes how we conceptualize and engage in relationship building and interactions in our qualitative research. This also provides space and opportunity for us to pause and come to know the research process, as well as revisit and revise previous perspectives on the research process.

Conclusion

Bella's has taught us that to create humane and affirming interactions for/with others in research spaces, we must have and engage spaces where our own humanity is affirmed. The more time and intention we invest in spaces where we find the freedom of full expression, the more tools and insight we have into how we might cultivate similar spaces for/with others. Cultivating and engaging in our onto-epistemological kinship space has invited us to see the intercentricity of the ontological and epistemological in the context of qualitative research. While the simultaneity and innateness of knowing and being comes as second nature in Bella's, we have to be more deliberate about leveraging those sensibilities in research relationships. Although it is not our individual or collective goal to re-create or reconstitute what we know as Bella's for any research project, we hope that the insights we have come to know and feel through our engagement in kinship and community can invite others to cultivate the types of relations, kinship, and community we can cocreate and sustain in our research endeavors.

References

Alexander, B. K. (2005). Embracing the teachable moment: The Black gay body in the classroom as embodied text. In E. P. Johnson & M. G. Henderson (Eds.), *Black queer theory: A critical anthology* (pp. 249–265). Duke University Press.

Allen, J. S. (2009). For "the children" dancing the beloved community. *Souls: A Critical Journal of Black Politics, Culture, and Society, 11*(3). https://doi.org/10.1080/10999940903088945

Bailey, M. M. (2013). *Butch queens up in pumps: Gender, performance, and ballroom culture in Detroit.* University of Michigan Press.

Baldwin, J. (2013). *The fire next time.* Vintage.

Bambara, T. C. (1980). *The salt eaters.* Vintage-Random.

Blockett, R. A. (2017). "I think it's very much placed on us": Black queer men laboring to forge community at a predominantly White and (hetero) cisnormative research institution. *International Journal of Qualitative Studies in Education, 30*(8), 800–816. https://doi.org/10.1080/09518398.2017.1350296

Blockett, R. A. (2018). *"We don't live in that world": Understanding the worldmaking practices of black queer graduate and undergraduate men at a predominately white and heterocisnormative midwestern research university* (Order No. 10750999) [Doctoral dissertation, Indiana University, Bloomington]. ProQuest Dissertations & Theses Global.

Boykin, K. (2005). *Beyond the down low: Sex, lies, and denial in Black America.* Carroll & Graf.

Cole, J. B., & Guy-Sheftall, B. (2003). *Gender talk: The struggle for women's equality in African American communities.* Ballantine.

Crawley, A. (2015). Otherwise, instituting. *Performance Research, 20*(4), 85–89. https://doi.org/10.1080/13528165.2015.1071043

Gill, L. K. (2012). Chatting back an epidemic: Caribbean gay men, HIV/AIDS, and the uses of erotic subjectivity. *GLQ: A Journal of Lesbian and Gay Studies, 18*(2–3), 277–295. https://doi.org/10.1215/10642684-1472899

Green, K. M. (2019). In the life: On Black queer kinship. *Women, Gender, and Families of Color, 7*(1), 98–101. https://muse.jhu.edu/article/733525

Harding, S. (1995). "Strong objectivity": A response to the new objectivity question. *Synthese, 104*(3), 331–349. https://doi.org/10.1007/BF01064504

Harris, J., & Njoku, N. (2017). Introduction. *International Journal of Qualitative Studies in Education, 30*(8), 707–710. https://doi.org/10.1080/09518398.2017.1353253

Hawkeswood, W. G. (1996). "Close to home": The organization of the gay scene in Harlem. In W. G. Hawkeswood & A. W. Costley (Eds.), *One of the children* (pp. 67–89). University of California Press.

Hurston, Z. N. (1937). *Their eyes were watching God.* Fawcett.

Lather, P. (1986). Issues of validity in openly ideological research: Between a rock and a soft place. *Interchange, 17*(4), 63–84. https://doi.org/ezproxy3.library.arizona.edu/10.1007/BF01807017

Lewis, M. M. (2011). Body of knowledge: Black queer feminist pedagogy, praxis, and embodied text. *Journal of Lesbian Studies, 15*(1), 49–57. https://doi.org/10.1080/10894160.2010.508411

Lorde, A. (1984). *Uses of the erotic: The erotic as power.* Kore.

Means, D. R., Beatty, C. C., Blockett, R. A., Bumbry, M., Canida, R. L., & Cawthon, T. W. (2017). Resilient scholars: Reflections from Black gay men on the doctoral journey. *Journal of Student Affairs Research and Practice, 54*(1), 109–120. https://doi.org/10.1080/19496591.2016.1219265

Mitchell, D. J., & Means, D. R. (2014). Quadruple consciousness: A literature review and new theoretical consideration for understanding the experiences of Black gay and bisexual college men at predominantly White institutions. *Journal of African American Males in Education, 5*(1), 23–35. https://jaamejournal.scholasticahq.com/article/18444.pdf

Mobley, S. D., Jr. (2017). Seeking sanctuary: (Re)Claiming the power of historically Black colleges and universities as places of Black refuge. *International Journal of Qualitative Studies in Education, 30*(10), 1036–1041. https://doi.org/10.1080/09518398.2017.1312593

Mobley, S. D., Jr., & Johnson, J. M. (2019). "No pumps allowed": The "problem" with gender expression and the Morehouse College "Appropriate Attire Policy." *Journal of Homosexuality, 66*(7), 867–895. https://doi.org/10.1080/00918369.2018.1486063

Mobley, S. D., Jr., McNally, T., & Moore, G. (2019). Revealing the potential for HBCUs to be liberatory environments for queer students. In E. M. Zamani-Gallaher, D. D. Choudhuri, & J. L. Taylor (Eds.), *Rethinking LGBTQIA students and collegiate contexts: Identity, policies, and campus climate* (pp. 99–119). Routledge.

Mobley S. D., Jr., Taylor, L. D., Jr., & Haynes, C. (2020). (Un) seen work: The pedagogical experiences of Black queer men in faculty roles. *International Journal of Qualitative Studies in Education, 33*(6), 604–620. https://doi.org/10.1080/09518398.2020.1747659

Nunokawa, J. (1991). "All the sad young men": AIDS and the age of mourning. *The Yale Journal of Criticism, 4*(2), 1.

Okello, W. K. (2020). "Loving flesh": Self-love, student development theory, and the coloniality of being. *Journal of College Student Development, 61*(6), 717–732. https:doi.org/10.1353/csd.2020.0071

Patel, L. (2014). Countering coloniality in educational research: From ownership to answerability. *Educational Studies, 50*(4), 357–377. https://doi.org/10.1080/00131946.2014.924942

Patton, L. D. (2018, November 15). Envisioning the "woke" academy [Presidential Address]. Association for the Study of Higher Education (ASHE) Conference, Tampa, FL, United States.

Shange, S. (2019). Play aunties and dyke bitches: Gender, generation, and the ethics of Black queer kinship. *The Black Scholar, 49*(1), 40–54. https://doi.org/10.1080/00064246.2019.1548058

Snipes, J. T. (Host). (2020, November). Legibility for what (No. 10) [Audio podcast episode]. *Blacktivism in the Academy*. The DREAM Collective & That Untitled Project. https://www.audible.com/pd/Blacktivism-In-the-Academy-Podcast/B08JJPM7YR

Stack, C. B. (1975). *All our kin: Strategies for survival in a black community*. Basic Books.

Stewart, D-L. (2016, September 8). Just because you are magic: A love letter to minoritized faculty in your first year. *Wilderness Voices: Speaking Truth to Power about Higher Ed and Society*. https://dlstewartradicalinsights.wordpress.com/2016/09/08/just-because-youre-magic-a-love-letter-to-minoritized-faculty-in-your-first-year/

Williams, V. (Writer), & Berlinger, J. (Director). (2014, July 13). Master class with Vanessa Williams [Television series episode]. In Harpo Studios (Producers), *Oprah's master class*. OWN.

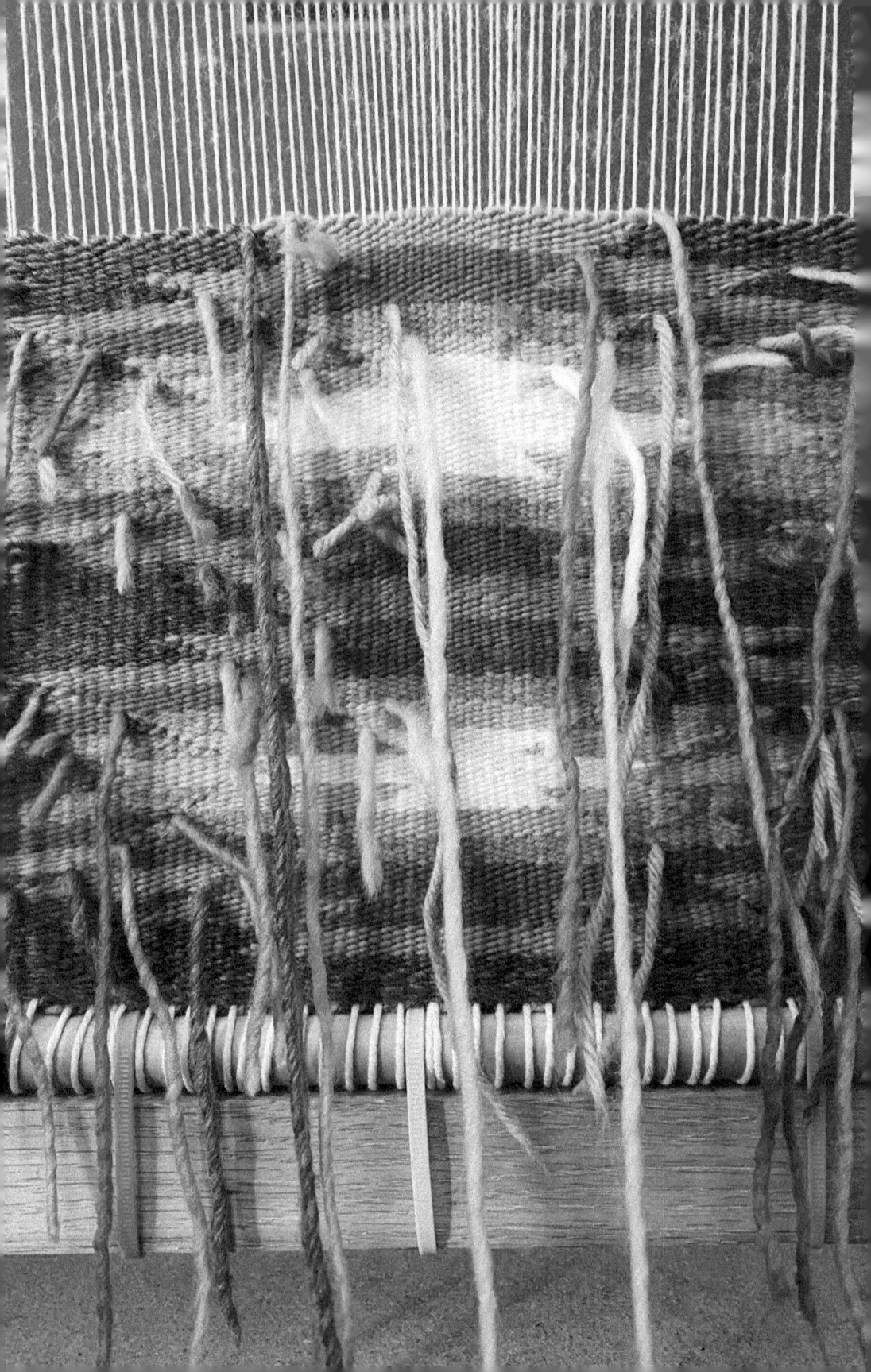

PART TWO

DURING

4

ARCHIVES IN THE HOLD

Overreading Black Student Activism

Zachary Brown

Black being's function within metaphysics is to inhabit the void of relationality.

—Warren (2018, p. 32)

He appears before us styled in a plain, light-colored button-down shirt, dark slacks, and black dress shoes. We know there is some form of debris dusted across his hair and surely across his face. It is perfectly contrasted with the dark, spirally tight curl pattern adorning his head, producing the facade of a compact 'fro. He is downcast in both look and spirit. And if not downcast in spirit, when he summons us inside his affective life, what does he reveal to us? Melancholy, rage, hope, despair, a cacophony of ambivalent emotion? His aesthetic urges us to ask if he is dressed up for an occasion. What is the occasion? Is it joyous? Morose? Bittersweet? Perhaps the event is the culmination of a series of staged, tactical movements. Or perhaps the event is no event at all—the repetition of narrative, a history that speaks in palindromic sequence—an echo of the nonevent of emancipation or Black freedom (Cunningham, 2017; Hartman, 1997).

We return to him again, adorned with a light (white?) button-down shirt, dark (black?) slacks, and his good shoes, you know, the ones you wear to church on Sunday. There is debris in his hair. (Maybe dirt? Dust?) It's perfectly contrasted with the familiar tight curls adorning his head. Though this time in our return to him he does not appear before us, he seemingly has never left. In this view, we now see a darkness staining his pristine white shirt. It is blood. Blood envelopes his shirt so much that the indelible task of deciphering the origin of the spill, the *mise-en-scène* of the photograph, lighting and color, confuses the moment. Where is the wound? What is the source of the wound? Who inflicted this wound? Is the young man attending to another's wound? Myriad questions surround this photograph, the scene, this archive. He looks down at the ground. If the camera locks eyes with him, doubly looking back at photographer and us as spectator, will our identifications with him, as we are hurled into the scene, be too much to bear? What happened after this moment? Before this moment? Is it strange to see him dressed up? As he dressed that morning, did he hear the nostalgic, tender nag from his mom reverberating in the air, "Hurry up and put on your church clothes so we can go! And you better put on your outside clothes as soon as we get back in the house!" He remembers that his mom isn't there though as the two officers sink their hands into his flesh, pinning his hands behind back, as he stands and surrenders his fatigued body. The officer is a nonevent,[1] a repetition of the incessant desire to capture Black body. The corners of his lips turn down, and the barrage of thoughts discordantly fill his mind. He thinks about his family. He thinks about the university as the authorizer of hope, the prayer for a better life and a better future. He wonders if his experience at college is changing him. Would he return home an Uncle Tom, Sam, shoe shining–type Negro[2]—a change that would thwart relation with self and (m)Other?[3] He reflects and ponders if his family will think about this moment of arrest and be shocked at his current precarious situation? Proud? Scared? Furious? Might his father's booming voice force any other sound out of the room, "We didn't send you there for all that; we sent you there to get a degree!" In the chaos of this photograph (Figure 4.1), it is as if time suspends forever. Black life, frozen in time, is suspended protest and riot.

---

[1] My use of *nonevent* is to suggest that the spectacularity of this scene of violence at San Francisco State College materialized in the arrest of this "man" exists to obfuscate the mundanity of anti-Black violence and position the violent scene as the locus of concern. Nonevent in this sense then speaks to the repetition of violence improperly named as an event (of police brutality) in and of itself. Martinot and Sexton's (2003) reflection on the everydayness of policing adds a clarification, asking, "But what are we doing when we demonstrate against police brutality, and find ourselves tacitly calling upon the government to help us do so? (p. 170). Wilderson's (2010) notes also prove helpful. In reference to the "common sense" discourse around police brutality and its focus on the spectacular, he notes this as a dismissal of the "everyday banality of White existence" (p. 141).

[2] These words are quoted from community member, activist, and only Black minister in the campus ministry association Hannibal Williams. Williams was speaking in the context of the radical tactics of the Black strikers and Black Student Union members whose practices often aligned with or were inspired by the local activist organizations such as the Western Addition Community Organization (WACO). For more context see Orrick (1969).

[3] For Lacan, the first intrapsychic relation an infant establishes is with the mother as Other (Homer, 2005) so that the (m)Other inaugurates all desiring for the psychic subject.

Figure 4.1. Newspaper photograph of two police officers arresting a man during the 1968 strike. Courtesy of the *San Francisco Observer* (1968) and San Francisco State Fine Arts Department.

Reading I: A Strike in Context

This photograph lives in the San Francisco State College Strike Collection. Now San Francisco State University (SFSU), this collection wrestles with "a campus erupted in turmoil" (J. Paul Leonard Library, n.d., para. 1). The turmoil the archive references primarily describes the series of intra-campus assaults on Black students and other "third-world" students throughout their tenure at the university. As the collection notes,

> San Francisco State became a focus for national attention on the needs of students of color as the campus erupted in turmoil. The SF State College Strike, also referred to as the Third World strike, embraced the concerns of minority students. During the Strike, faculty groups, student groups, off-campus participants, and others inundated the campus community with broadsides and leaflets announcing points of view. (para. 1)

Narratively, this collection describes the history-making strike (in both its duration and the tactics applied) at the college, culminating in the issuance of 10 formal demands by the Black Student Union (BSU), the formation of the coalitional body of the Third World Liberation Front (TWLF), and the emergence of a university college dedicated to the founding principles of the movement. This strike (against racism, imperialism, and capitalism) by the BSU responding to the necrotic ecologies of campus living, local San Francisco and Bay Area politics, and a conservative California state created a lasting impact on the history of SFSU, surrounding universities, and the capacity for student mobilization and organization across the country. It is no surprise then that the San Francisco State College strike, one of the longest student strikes in the United States, has caught the attention of various scholars (Barlow & Shapiro, 1971; Biondi, 2012; Cohen, 2013; Horowitz, 1986; I. Rogers, 2012; I. H. Rogers, 2012; Smith et al., 1970). The official duration of the TWLF strike is documented as lasting between November 6, 1968, and March 21, 1969. Comprised of the BSU, the Native American Students Union, the Mexican American Student Confederation, Latin American Student Organization (LASO), La Raza, the Philippine (now Pilipino) American Collegiate Endeavor (PACE), the Intercollegiate Chinese for Social Action (ICSA), and later the Asian American Political Alliance, this coalition of students destabilized commonsense education—education that devalued but categorically evaded minoritarian knowledge production. The results of this campus movement engendered the formation of not only the first Black Studies program in the United States, but subsequent disciplinary formations that attended to the third world and postcolonial subject and moves toward a politic of coalition within racial/ethnic groups and campus activism that would span the next few decades (Broadhurst, 2014; Lye, 2010; Morgan & Davis, 2019; Rojas, 2007).

This strike stirred not only the San Francisco community, but even radiated beyond the campus, eschewing activism through the state of California from then acting governor Ronald Reagan, and even admonishment of the movement from the office of the then 37th president of the United States, Richard Nixon. Indeed, San Francisco State College illuminated a scene of violence where students were entangled in campus struggle(s), and yet what made this strike so notable was that it was informed through logics developed outside of the college. For example, we cannot separate the tactical position of the students as parallel with the political education occurring in the local Fillmore community. This is of no surprise, as George Mason Murray,[4] a recently fired graduate student

---

[4] The decision to fire George Mason Murray as a teaching assistant, prompted by the board of trustees, was engendered by various speeches such as one at Fresno State calling for the end of U.S. imperialism in Vietnam or a speech perhaps too close to home at San Francisco State College advocating the need for armed struggle in campus autonomy by slaying "slavemasters." For more see Karaguezian (1971) and Orrick (1969).

instructor, was also the minister of education for the Black Panther Party. Even within a cursory glance then, we see that concerns of the Black students on campus were not just a response to the anti-Black policies and actions by administrators at San Francisco State College but spoke to broader concerns around Black social and political life. This point is further elucidated by the assassination of Martin Luther King, Jr. earlier that year, in April 1968. In this way, the tenuous nature of emancipation and freedom discourse, as thought through the larger discourse on civil rights, would have us not only think about the aims of the Black Panther Party in the context of the formation of Black studies and the broader Black revolutionary struggle for self-determination and campus autonomy, but also question the purchase of yoking Black political agency as constitutive of Black subjectivity. Or, put another way, through depictions of Black students as simply agents of resistance transforming these structures through collective activity, what assumptions are being made about the scope of Black sociality as a (non)relation to state and civil society? The liberal rights of man—liberty, individuality, and justice—engendered through de jure freedom, act as rhetorical screen that must be abraded by new ways of seeing.

Reading II: Archive(s) in the Afterlife of Slavery

> *Whenever we set out to answer the properly historicist questions of who did what, where, and when, we inevitably end up making theoretical claims about the who in question, claims that imply or assert a theory of the subject—in this case, a subject whose political actions and utterances are reflections of a self-conscious will and desire.*

—Kazanjian (2015, p. 81)

San Francisco State College has a series of collections that capture Black struggle, the formation of Black studies and the evolution of an inchoate Black social, which is to say activist-oriented, life on campus. I designate the series of collections that document this period as the TWLF archive. I use this term to highlight not only its cultural significance to higher education, but also to reveal the conditions that would make these terms coherent and clear rather than another site of "confounded identities" (Spillers, 1987, p. 65) that mark the Black "woman" a point of confusion, pleasure, and ambiguity—and further, that this precarious position of those designated as Black "women," in the current social and symbolic order, has devastating consequences for those marked as Black female *and* Black male subjects. My use of *male* and *female* is an attempt to maneuver within and outside of gender as a(n) en/fore/closure that attempts to plot fixed coordinates of liberal *man* and *woman* onto Blackness. In accordance with Spillers, my use of (fe)male forces us to contend with ungendered flesh in its "seared, divided, ripped-apartness," a life form "riveted to the ship's hole, fallen, or 'escaped' overboard" (p. 67). Put this way, Black male flesh as susceptible to the same violent ungendering presents an urgent dilemma in how we might think about Black revolutionary struggle on campus as the territory of brothers,[5] but in this fraternal domain we are also posed to interrogate even representations of Black strike leaders. Moreover, the terror that would steal and transform African persons from Indigenous homelands into fungible flesh throws into crisis the borrowed grammars of *student* and *activist* so that any protocols that contend with Black life must be adequately disassembled without the thrust for reconfiguration. Thus, we might ask, "What is the (third) world, and how does Black male flesh inhabit this space? What conditions might make a (third) world possible in relation to the modern, which is to say, imperial university?"[6] And if, as la paperson (2017) dreams, a third university is possible, does Black flesh not provide the blueprint for its (meta) physical architecture? And, if we can understand the university archive as a technology of power, does representation of Black life in the archive as it is yoked to agency and resistance yield another crisis?

The archive as a function of power as well as a critical methodology has been taken up by myriad scholars encouraging us to interrogate and shift how we construct and think about archives and archiving as a method (Hartman, 2007, 2008; Stoler, 2009; Trouillot, 1995). The digital archive as mode of engagement also requires equal attention in unthinking the onto-epistemic violence imputed in histories of colonialism, imperialism, and empire that claim to know Black subjectivity (Lowe, 2015). As Dillon (2017) poignantly noted, "The new availability of digital archival material gives the coloniality of archives additional fuel and force, particularly when we imagine the archives as sources from which to simply draw information" (p. 250). Thus, among the central concerns of many historians and scholars of Black life, and this specific chapter, is contending again and always what it means to live with and within the vestiges of slavery. The "history" in question in this chapter is not how Black students made advances within/against the university, but of how those marked as Black, whether participants in university life or not, condition a relation to/against the broader social body that is simultaneously exacerbated through and drowned out by the noise of emancipation. Put another way, Black freedom as a nonevent corroborates the preservation of absence—the nonrelation of Black life within the social sphere, the nonexistence of and never existing within the social and relational structure

---

[5] I'm trying to call attention here to the invisibilization of Black women's labor in the revolutionary struggle through the synonymity of Black Power with Black brotherhood.

[6] For more on the relationship between the university, imperialism, and campus dissent see Chatterjee and Maira (2014).

of society. The task of making sense of Black life becomes fraught in that entering the archive to make sense of Black life across various geo-histories simultaneously denudes a capacious reading of the lives we desire to know. As Hartman (2007) reminded us, the desire to recover these moments of disruption of wanton violence implicate us all—making us "guilty as the rest" in trying to save the young man at the center of a chapter from "oblivion" (p. 137).

What methodological approach, then, might assist in tempering my own desire—to find, locate, name, make sense of violence; to redeem violence of the Black male body in the TWLF archive? Instead, what relation must be insisted as it concerns the representational violence of the archive in order to tarry with Black male flesh as a possible space for theorizing Black masculine subjectivities? And to approach this, if I even/ever can, perhaps, I first might ask, "What must I know and assume about my*self*?" My relation to my own errant *flight* of masculinities—failed, appropriated, cited?

I care about him though I do not know him. It feels like I am writing to him. Telling him "I see you" and "I'm sorry for what this world does to you." Perhaps then this chapter can function as not only an epistolary gesture as I write to him, about him, and for him, but also as a method of writing a different relation, a way to "defend the dead" and those living social death as Sharpe (2016) introduced. In this way, the least important "fact" from this archival investigation we might glean about him is the moniker "student activist." Instead, I suggest we turn toward confounding identities that converge and collide during this strike in this young Black man's life. This turn then marks the occasion to overread (Kazanjian, 2015) the material in the TWLF archive and speculate about these various scenes, being mindful of the constant threat of "imputed subjectivity" (p. 81) that stifles through archival representation. I mobilize overreading in this capacity to relieve the presuppositional desires for the reconstitution of higher education projected onto the Black strike leaders. Further, I argue that overreading helps us hold the fact that the tactics exhibited during the strike assuredly changed the landscape of higher education forever, and yet recorded memory, particularly as it is mediated by the university archive, affords little credibility in articulating the actualities of Black will and desire as such. If we situate the colonial college (Wilder, 2013) alongside the "notion that colonial states were first and foremost information-hungry machines in which power accrued from the massive accumulation of ever-more knowledge" (Stoler, 2002, p. 100) within an affective economy that recognized some "sentiments and civilities" as "expert colonial knowledge that endowed some persons with the credentials to generate trustworthy truth-claims" (p. 101) a significant problem emerges. I argue that this program arises precisely in the moment that Black male flesh is recovered (represented) in the archive as the Black male (agentic) body that *desires* to transform the campus. My methodological practice of overreading in this context tries to relieve the obscuring presence of agency yoked to institutional desire by suggesting that the sentiments and civilities that underwrite our understanding of the archival representation of this historic scene of campus violence and change must always belie Black desire. What is most deceptive or obscuring about the archives of student activism is that it is read against the university; it is cast within a counter-university context. These counter-university contexts are deeply important; however, as they simultaneously insert claims about Black resistance and agency, they move us away from the opportunity to read along the archival grain, to privilege the analysis of the archive as a process invested in producing regimes of *truth* to overread "for its consistencies of misinformation, omission, and mistake" (p. 100). Why might we rely on the TWLF (counter-)political claims about Black agency? Or about Black desire in relation to the university? By centering the direct practices of the Black strike leaders, we disrupt dominant and counter-hegemonic claims about the nature of Black student activism or the integrity of the "student activist" and "activist" position writ large. Put another way, how might overreading Black life allow for us to imagine different horizons that evade the university's gaze?

Reading III: Occasion to Overread

Blackness marks the occasion to overread. To start with Black thought evacuates our assumptions about the TWLF and its archival contents to pose a different set of questions about Black life insofar as Black life can be *genuinely* thought as a thinking toward Blackness (Sexton, 2012). What does it mean to defend the dead and dying in a project that desires to convey the institution of higher education as an architect of Black suffering in both theory and praxis, in philosophy and spirit? To whom and to what am I responsible in carving out space to recognize Black living as a fugitive act in the longue durée of anti-Blackness? As a scholar bound to an institution of higher education, where institutional care is a reformation of anti-Black violence, what are the ethical limits and boundaries to this project? Aligned with Sharpe's (2016) notions of thinking care as a problem for thought and an unyielding commitment to defend the dead and dying as central in my approach to method, I approach my archival research as a journey with Black student activists across multiple different times and spaces, as an occasion to overread.

The notion that we find him within a special collection authorized through a university, a process of officialization, marks the occasion to overread. Or, put differently, the digital contents of the collection and what I extend as the TWLF archive exist insofar as staff have the capacity within the institution to document, date, and archive material—material that is deemed relevant and that staff then offer to the public. The capacity to even offer up this material is fraught if we consider the labor extracted from chattel slavery, Native genocide, and land dispossession (Carney, 1999; King, 2019; Wilder, 2013) as what made possible the physical manifestations of educational institutions. I pose thinking Black fungibility in relationship to the university as the quintessential, unanswerable, and unthought question that inaugurated the knowledge economy. This swirling economy embodied through "degree-granting" institutions operates as another lens through which anti-Black violence is enacted. Though this is not the intent of the chapter, it is worth posing the question of how, across disciplines, conferred degrees have the potential to aid in the maintenance and sustainment of anti-Blackness (e.g., social work/psychology, education programs, STEM, arts, sociology, and criminal justice programs). I highlight this to the scale of anti-Blackness and its structuring of the modern university. Though this chapter is far from offering a genealogy of the dark philosophies undergirding higher education, we might do well to revisit some of the philosophical questions about the aim and purpose of higher education, the goal and function of the university in relation to state and civil society. The university needs Blackness, which is to say anti-Blackness. The TWLF archive therein might function as a repository for anti-Black musings and machinations, an extension of the hold of the ship, of the plantation. Stated differently, the archive is a reflection of the power relations that constructed, one, the universal/university subject (White, cisheterosexual man), and two, the (nonhuman) racial Other as the fulcrum in which the different possibilities, or rather possibilities of difference (e.g., gender and sexuality), are fully, liminally, and impossibly elaborated. And this power relation ensconces itself as anti-Blackness in the weather, the totality of (campus) climate (Sharpe, 2016). In this way, overreading each encounter with officialized material from the TWLF archive should be thought of as an opening to the door of no return (Brand, 2012). That "place, real, imaginary and imagined," a site of deep ambivalence, of theft and dislocation as Diasporic inheritance, holding both the ongoing terror of death and captivity and within this same "cognitive schema . . . rebellions, emancipations, political struggles" (Brand, 2012, p. 21). Sharpe (2012) clarifies the point well:

> That un/known door is the frame that produces black bodies as signifiers of enslavement and its (unseeable) excesses; it is the beginning, the ontology, of the black. It is the ground that positions black bodies to bear the burden of that signification, and that positions some black people to know and embrace it. (para. 7)

The importance of the door as figurative and real then allows for a heightened sense of sight—an ocular stronghold from where we can finally place the stalwart question of (be)longing and relation(ality).

Upon opening this door, a third time, we see more clearly his name, Don McAllister.[7] On the horizon though, is Black male flesh ungendered, unseeable excess but now perhaps something more. To tarry with unseeable excess for a moment is to also acknowledge this him and the function of the photograph in Black visual culture. Photography captures moments ad infinitum. These depictions of anti-Black violence and suffering sedimented in the cache of visual culture are sutured to White jouissance, the inexorable economy surplus enjoyment (Lacan, 1968/2007; Marriott, 2000). The photograph of Don McAllister shows us the spectacle and spectacular nature of anti-Black violence in the constitution of a Black subject so that we might dare to ask how this young man comes into being through this photograph. If through a vantage point of visual suffering, an inchoate Black student activist identity and political agency emerges, it seems, rather, only through the spectacle of violence, gratuitous or quotidian, Black students are interpellated into the university.

Reading IV: Black Lacuna

In the fourth view, holding onto this knowledge, he may appear to us differently. He's the center of the scene, the compositional focal point. He awakens in us a strange macabre curiosity: the inescapable desire to look at the scene of a crash; that thing that outweighs the risk of looking itself; what one might miss if they refuse to look; a seeing pleasure so great that the coordinates of the collision are displaced within the spatial and temporal frame of the photograph and are (re)mapped onto his literal and figurative body. He is the embodiment of wreckage, of carnality and corporeal terror, insofar as the university archive treats him as a *gendered subject*. I suggest then gender, not as additive to how we might come to understand him as a "terror," or as terror producing, but as an extension of, and technology through which, anti-Blackness becomes legible. Thus, the network of signifiers—man, male,

---

[7] It wasn't until later that I came across the name of the man in the photograph. This photograph was captured on December 3, 1968, on Bloody Tuesday. A different bloodied picture of Don McAllister appears earlier in the campus newspaper, *The Gater*, in their December 4 issue. It matters that in that initial publication, he was described as a "battered prisoner." While revealing his name at this point in this chapter should corroborate humanity (he is someone's son), it is important to state that taking on the name "battered prisoner" further exposes the relationship between Black self-determination and the university.

and masculine—signal an interconnectedness that converges at a single Black point—a relational void. And if I think from this point as an entry into the loss of signification, where signification is no longer called to duty, a way to feel through the apex of fleshly activity, Black male flesh ungendered is illumined. This, again, is the intractable task of clearing the field of static. Tasked so with this indelible (gender) tension, I believe it is worth expanding on how we might think from the missing parts, from unfillable space, or the "void," as Warren (2018) might describe it.

If Blackness as absence enables the presence of humanity, of being in the world, I want to think through this absence as Black *lacuna*. Black lacuna as a mode of studying Black life under the threat of absolute erasure and domination takes up the void of Black being, as the veritable space of infinite potentiality and possibility for those living social death. Black lacuna as a method resists the desire of plenitude in relation to Blackness and feels for multiple fragments of a thing not quite legible, but indeed rich and sonorous. Black lacuna thinks of looking and hearing as appositional processes to suggest a methodologically sensate (over)reading. In this way, looking invites the sonic register as another helpful strategy in archival method so that we can *hear* these images. As Tina Campt (2017) suggested, attuning oneself to the sensory and affective protocols in analyzing photography of Black persons may help "perceive their quiet frequencies of possibility" (p. 45). Looking then indexes an ocular protocol that resists this gaze and White image but instantiates a gesture toward the prioritization of knowledge alien to the eye and intimate with aural and sonic frequencies. What I suggest here is that by attending to this tension, and refusing to use this archival encounter as constitutive of a Black political agency, methodological certainty (and with it, relation to the TWLF archive) is a myth that only speculation can keep alive. The desire to create subjects out of violence, or to use violence as the fulcrum in the configuration of Black (student) subjectivity effaces a critical viewing of this photograph. Critically viewing this photograph and TWLF archival material requires a cognizance of our own gaze, as a mode of capture, as a form of pleasure in which we all find ourselves implicated. Critical viewing recognizes this moment not as an impasse, but in shifting our relationship to looking the need for multiple different methods for engaging Black life in the archive is augmented. Black life—arrested in the archive—is ocular trauma, the "both/and" of ascertaining the full scope of Black diasporic life via official archival material and the scopophilic pleasure derived from *taking in* the "nightmare" (Jackson, 2011) of Black flesh. To commune with the dead and those living social death is to surrender to risk and uncertainty and forge something anew in the narration of Black life in and outside of the archive. On the horizon, then, of this dark (non)space, Black lacuna is always already a trace of something like and altogether different from the autoethnographic—the ongoing imbrication of multiple, fragmented selves always in relation and reflexivity.

References

Barlow, W., & Shapiro, P. (1971). *An end to silence: The San Francisco State College student movement in the 60s*. Pegasus.

Biondi, M. (2012). *The Black revolution on campus*. University of California Press.

Brand, D. (2012). *A map to the door of no return: Notes to belonging*. Vintage Canada.

Broadhurst, C. (2014). Campus activism in the 21st century: A historical framing. In C. J. Broadhurst & G. L. Martin (Eds.), *"Radical Academia"? Understanding the Climates for Campus Activists* (New Directions for Higher Education, no. 167, pp. 3–15). Jossey-Bass. https://doi.org/10.1002/he.20101

Campt, T. M. (2017). *Listening to images*. Duke University Press.

Carney, C. M. (1999). *Native American higher education in the United States*. Transaction.

Chatterjee, P., & Maira, S. (2014). *The imperial university: Academic repression and scholarly dissent*. University of Minnesota Press.

Cohen, R. (2013). *Rebellion in black and white: Southern student activism in the 1960s*. Johns Hopkins University Press.

Cunningham, N. (2017). The nonarrival of Black freedom (c. 12.6.84). *Women & Performance: A Journal of Feminist Theory, 27*(1), 112–120. https://doi.org/10.1080/0740770X.2017.1282097

Dillon, E. M. (2017). Translatio studii and the poetics of the digital archive: Early American literature, Caribbean assemblages, and freedom dreams. *American Literary History, 29*(2), 248–266. https://doi.org/10.1093/alh/ajx007

Hartman, S. V. (1997). *Scenes of subjection: Terror, slavery, and self-making in nineteenth century America*. Oxford University Press.

Hartman, S. V. (2007). *Lose your mother: A journey along the Atlantic slave route*. Farrar, Straus and Giroux.

Hartman, S. (2008). Venus in two acts. *Small Axe, 28*(2), 1–14. https://muse.jhu.edu/article/241115

Homer, S. (2005). *Jacques Lacan* (1st ed.). Routledge.

Horowitz, H. L. (1986). The 1960s and the transformation of campus cultures. *History of Education Quarterly, 26*, 1–38.

Jackson, Z. (2011). Waking nightmares—on David Marriott. *GLQ: A Journal of Lesbian and Gay Studies, 17*(2–3), 357–363. https://doi.org/10.1215/10642684-1163445

J. Paul Leonard Library. (n.d.). *SF State College Strike Collection*. https://library.sfsu.edu/sf-state-strike-collection

Karaguezian, D. (1971). *Blow it up! The Black student revolt at San Francisco State and the emergence of Dr. Hayakawa*. Gambit.

Kazanjian, D. (2015). Scenes of speculation. *Social Text, 125*, 77–84. https://doi-org.ezproxy3.library.arizona.edu/10.1215/01642472-3315778

King, T. L. (2019). *The Black shoals: Offshore formations of Black and Native studies*. Duke University Press.

Lacan, J. (2007). *The seminar of Jacques Lacan book XVII: The other side of psychoa-nalysis* (R. Grigg, Trans.). Duke University Press. (Original work published 1968)

la paperson. (2017). *A third university is possible.* University of Minnesota Press.

Lowe, L. (2015). *The intimacies of four continents.* Duke University Press.

Lye, C. (2010). US ethnic studies and third worldism, 40 years later. *Inter-Asia Cultural Studies, 11*(2), 188–193. https://doi.org/10.1080/14649371003616128

Marriott, D. (2000). *On Black men.* Edinburgh University Press.

Martinot, S., & Sexton, J. (2003). The avant-garde of white supremacy. *Social Identities, 9*(2), 169–181. https://doi.org/10.1080/1350463032000101542

Morgan, D. L., & Davis, C. H. F. (2019). *Student activism, politics, and campus climate in higher education.* Routledge.

Orrick, W. H., Jr. (1969). *Shut it down! A college in crisis: San Francisco State College, October 1968–April 1969.* National Commission on the Causes and Prevention of Violence.

Rogers, I. (2012). The Black campus movement and the institutionalization of Black studies, 1965–1970. *Journal of African American Studies, 16*(1), 21–40. https://link.springer.com/article/10.1007/s12111-011-9173-2

Rogers, I. H. (2012). *The Black campus movement: Black students and the racial reconstitution of higher education, 1965–1972.* Palgrave McMillan.

Rojas, F. (2007). *From Black power to Black studies: How a radical social movement became an academic discipline.* Johns Hopkins University Press.

San Francisco Observer. (1968). *Newspaper photograph of two police officers arresting a man during the 1968 strike.* SF State College Strike Collection, Fine Arts Department at San Francisco State University. https://diva.sfsu.edu/collections/strike/bundles/210902

Sexton, J. (2012). Ante-anti-Blackness: Afterthoughts. *Lateral, 1*(1). http://csalateral.org/section/theory/ante-anti-blackness-afterthoughts-sexton/

Sharpe, C. (2012). Response to "ante-anti-Blackness." *Lateral, 1*(1). https://csalateral.org/issue/1/ante-anti-blackness-response-sharpe/

Sharpe, C. E. (2016). *In the wake: On Blackness and being.* Duke University Press.

Smith, R., Axen, R., & Pentony, D. (1970). *By any means necessary: The revolutionary struggle at San Francisco State.* Jossey-Bass.

Spillers, H. J. (1987). Mama's baby, papa's maybe: An American grammar book. *diacritics, 17*(2), 65–81. https://doi.org/10.2307/464747

Stoler, A. L. (2002). *Carnal knowledge and imperial power: Race and the intimate in colonial rule.* University of California Press.

Stoler, A. L. (2009). *Along the archival grain: Epistemic anxieties and colonial common sense.* Princeton University Press.

Trouillot, M. (1995). *Silencing the past: Power and the production of history.* Beacon.

Warren, C. L. (2018). *Ontological terror: Blackness, nihilism, and emancipation.* Duke University Press.

Wilder, C. S. (2013). *Ebony and ivy: Race, slavery, and the troubled history of America's universities.* Bloomsbury.

Wilderson, F. B. (2010). *Red, white and black: Cinema and the structure of U.S. antagonisms.* Duke University Press.

5

HEEDING HAUNTINGS IN RESEARCH FOR MATTERING

Irene H. Yoon and Grace A. Chen

A s students, educators, and researchers, we (Irene and Grace) sometimes feel in touch with a generative force that cannot be recorded well in our data. These hauntings defy empirical logic: what is nonmaterial is not necessarily immaterial; what is evident is not necessarily factual. Hauntology reflects not just the topic of research or inquiry (i.e., not all research has to be about ghosts, but it very well may be); hauntology reflects how the research is undertaken, how the researcher is transformed, and how different, multiple ways of knowing and mattering are part of making the past and future.

In this chapter, we write about haunting as a research process, shaping our dreams, epistemologies, coding, purpose, and engagement. We heed hauntings with some structural and stylistic exploration—musical fugue, philosophy, dictionary definitions, Greek chorus, research questions, and conversation, leaving traces in the footnotes (Gómez-Barris & Gray, 2010). Our goal is to share essences of haunting and hauntology, leaving openings for your own ghosts.[1]

What We Mean When We Say *Ghosts*

Ghosts expand our hauntological imaginations to truths beyond what has been permitted. Here we define hauntings that tap into affective and uncanny dimensions of epistemology.

---

[1] Throughout, we have cited sources that represent a tiny sip of these heterogeneous rememories in multiple academic disciplines, fiction genres, nonfiction essays and interviews, and popular songs.

Ghost *(n.).*[2] *An incorporeal force that is dead but returns to and interrupts awareness of the living such that it is present for futures. A "paradoxical" (Derrida, 1994) "absent presence" (Gordon, 2008) that is structurally and materially produced, yet intangible. Synonyms: apparition, ghoul, haunt, phantom, revenant, shadow, specter, spirit, visitation.*

While ghosts are heterogeneous in affect, desires and intentions, and histories, they are and were all targets of oppression and victims of state-sanctioned violence that has been submerged. For individuals and families, they may never be spoken of; for researchers, they may only be inferred in formal documents and recorded narratives. Ghosts push us to remember, to correct the record, and thus make it possible to do something different and better for the past and future (Derrida, 1994; Gill & Erevelles, 2017; Hartman, 2008, 2019). In doing so, ghosts present a "something-to-be-done" to those they haunt (Gordon, 2008).

Haunting *(n.). An experience or sensation of knowledge or familiarity without prior exposure or access to them; the uncanny (Freud, 2003). A process of return and revisitation of the past to the present; a rejection of linear-sequential time. An act of such return by ghosts. A memory of and ongoing agitation about injustice(s).*[3]

Being haunted is not a metaphor (Cho, 2008; Lincoln & Lincoln, 2015). Being haunted is to be repeatedly visited by multisensory and affective evidence of spirits who are not alive and not quite dead; who are silenced or hidden; who are actively unremembered. Haunting is a process of distorting and repeating time that is instigated by violence and challenges boundaries around reality and possibility. Here, at the edge of what you knew and will have had to understand, ghosts haunt witnesses (Derrida, 1994; Gómez-Barris & Gray, 2010).

Ghost *(n.). "It is something that one does not know, precisely, and one does not know if precisely it is, if it exists, if it responds to a name and corresponds to an essence. One does not know: not out of ignorance, but because this non-object, this non-present present, this being-there of an absent or departed one no longer belongs to knowledge. At least no longer to that which one*

---

[2] Format inspired by "A Glossary of Haunting" (Tuck & Ree, 2013).

[3] "And I, I am feeling a little peculiar" (Perry, 1992, 1:05).

"Its quietude was anything but simple. It was the kind of quiet that is in no way an absence. It is fulsome and expressive. Restless, awkward, and unsettling, it is a form of quiet where gnawing questions simmer and send one searching for more complicated answers (Campt, 2017, p. 18).

thinks one knows by the name of knowledge. . . . Here is—or rather there is, over there, an unnameable or almost unnameable thing: something between something and someone, anyone or anything" (Derrida, 1994, p. 5).

Names matter, but names as claimed and given by ancestors are different from names that are labels in disguise. Labels contain, flatten, constrain, and stamp documentation. Ghosts are knowledges, nonbeings, that resist this kind of oppression. You and your ghosts are changing and renaming all the time; ghosts pushing beyond change seek more just futures.

Future *(n.). A time that is yet to come and is a point along the way to more times to come. A space-time that is neither now nor past, yet has the traces of both (the metaphor of space for time is not a metaphor). For ghosts, futures may have existed and passed already. Related: futurity.*[4]

Ghosts seem confined to past and present; they were never intended to have futures or dreams. Futurity requires

the [verb] tense of possibility that grammarians refer to as the future real conditional or *that which will have **had to** happen*. The grammar of black feminist futurity is a performance of a future that hasn't yet happened but must. It is an attachment to a belief in what should be true, which impels us to realize that aspiration. . . . It's a politics of pre-figuration that involves living the future now. (Campt, 2017, p. 17, emphasis in original)

The "future real conditional" means dreams must change as the future becomes. Some dreams are nightmares. Past dreams—some forgotten, some foregone—are some of the ghosts that haunt us.

How to Know if You're Being Haunted

Someday you be walking down the road and you hear something or see something going on. So clear. And you think it's you thinking it up. A thought picture. But no. It's when you bump into a rememory that belongs to somebody else. . . . The picture is still there and what's more, if you go

---

[4] While there are a variety of conceptualizations and disciplines that are concerned with temporality and futures, futurisms, and futurities, we draw from queer crip time (Kafer, 2013), sociological haunting (Gordon, 2008, 2011), and Black feminist futurities (Campt, 2017). We also examine implicit explorations of futurity through ideas of reconciliation (Wale et al., 2020; Whitlinger, 2020). These all are related to, but differ from, Afrofuturism, futurism, Indigenous futures, and critical temporality studies.

there—you who never was there—if you go there and stand in the place where it was, it will happen again; it will be there for you, waiting for you. (Morrison, 1987, p. 36)

Bumping into "a rememory that belongs to somebody else" means that ghosts do not only haunt those who have been direct targets of institutional violence. Ghosts also haunt those who could have been targets but weren't; they haunt those who work in the institutions, who inflict pain and have come to be aware of it. The legacies of slavery and settler colonialism—the two parents of the United States' brand of White supremacy and capitalism, cis-heteropatriarchy, misogyny, and ableism—live on and have borne many descendants in research. People who have experienced pain and oppression by state-sponsored institutions already know these ghosts. Communing with spirits may come more easily to some researchers than to others, but it can be learned if you know how to wander.

Hauntings are like musical fugues, where phrases are repeated, overlapping, woven together into a more complex sequence. Ghosts plant questions, images, sounds, words, or dreams that appear over and over in varying patterns. A fugue repeats, but it has a direction. Following are the phrases in our haunting fugue.

Phrase 1: Hauntings Are Processes of Institutionalized, State-Sanctioned Violence

While individuals can have histories with violence, haunting is primarily about state-sanctioned, institutional violence (Cho, 2008; Lincoln & Lincoln, 2015; Schwab, 2010; Wale et al., 2020). Institutional violence leaves affective and material traces—on perpetrators, on victims, on land, on time—though not equally, and not in the same ways (Schwab, 2010; Wale et al., 2020). Like erasing pencil, some impression remains in the paper, and the surface of the paper becomes fuzzier. You cannot quite make out the words that used to be written there, even though you can physically feel their impressions. Both pasts and futures are erased through state-sanctioned violence; from the present, there are possibilities that we cannot imagine because they have been foreclosed even before they could be dreamed (Crawley, 2018; Wale et al., 2020).

Assaults on personhood and on persons' bodies are "coded in" to structures (e.g., bridges too narrow or too low hanging for buses to pass; admissions policies; discourses about "high" and "low" students; student information databases). Violence inhabits zoning, housing, dress, health, tax, software programs, and building codes. Ghosts remember the daily toll of physical, cognitive, and emotional exhaustion that it takes to navigate these codes. A first trace of institutional, state-sanctioned violence is silencing and erasure, which ironically often coincides with hyperdocumentation and regulation (Gill & Erevelles, 2017). Research codes, too, structure our interpretations of data (MacLure, 2013). Although coding is a structure of ableist White colonizer research (Dolmage, 2018), coding is also embedded in our thinking (it's codes all the way down, as generations of anthropologists have to unlearn). So what will your research code, decode, uncode, or recode? What does it not code at all?

> *There are students you can't forget—when you feel like you did everything you could, but the school system consumed them anyway. You know you (and everyone around you) failed them, but you're mystified at what else anyone in your position could have done. You aren't sure what happened to them after they left your class or school. You could feel a power in them, but it didn't know where to go. And so you remember them. You recognize traces of them in other students. You talk about them, revisit stories where they starred in some event or other.*
>
> *Who are you again in this story, the haunted or the haunting?*

A second trace of institutionalized violence is when any single individual isn't necessarily a perpetrator, but also is one, in everyday erosions of dignity and love. Often, state-sanctioned violence is committed because someone in the institution is following codes and protocols, making little room for response or reconciliation. Institutional actors commit assaults from ambiguous positions. Are they aware of doing harm, and to what extent are they responsible for it (Hong, 2014)? Institutional actors are themselves vulnerable to disposability. We are not here to judge, but there are futures where we will have had to reckon with responsibility.

> *You wish you had done many different things. You think of these when you and your students sparkle. You invite these memories to your councils, your meetings, your consciousness. Spirits flit through your everyday routines, whispering and tilting realities in the direction of more just possibilities.*

As educators, it is impossible not to be haunted by inflicting the violence of schooling. Likewise, as researchers, it is impossible not to be complicit with inflicting the violence of research. We feel this painful truth, tasting the bitterness of our experiences of erasure in the same institutions.

Phrase 2: Ghosts Use Repetition in Haunting

In *Spectres of Marx*, Derrida (1994) began his discussion of spectrality with the line, "The time is out of joint" (p. xxi) from Shakespeare's *Hamlet*. Derrida repeated this sentence throughout the text to examine disjunctures when ghosts return to presence, but not to being. Ghosts move independent of time and space, and thereby disrupt space–time relationships, the myth that linear chronological time and tangibility constitute reality (Gordon, 2008; cf. Kafer, 2013). With state-sanctioned violence, we may doubt the reliability of what we remember (J.W. Scott, 1991).

Paradoxically, while ghosts return from the past, haunting is replete with futurity (Gordon, 2011). We may anticipate ghosts' return and may try to avoid or predict their appearance, for ghosts were not intended to have had futures; their pasts were not recorded as if they would make progress toward a worthwhile future memory (Gordon, 2011; cf. Kafer, 2013). But ghosts left unacknowledged will repeat and repeat; they have time to remember. That is, hauntings are the result of unsuccessful attempts at silencing—"seething" reappearances of feelings and violence that were presumed or desperately hoped to have been left behind (Gordon, 2008). Haunted visitations shake empirical certainties unpredictably but repeatedly through flashbacks: déjà vu of things we cannot have known or places we have never been, a breeze on our skin or a scent that no one else can feel or smell.[5]

Phrase 3: By Haunting, Ghosts Change Belief

We are haunted by holes that leave gaps in too many of us researchers (*how far back in the past does the future begin?*).[6] Ghosts may not be truly free; they spread their dreams, seeding our imaginations, sleep, and senses with their desires and memories (Cho, 2008; Gordon, 2008; Lincoln & Lincoln, 2015). Their boundlessness is terrifying to people committed to sanity (*they have followed us here, where we had no past*).

By returning to haunt, ghosts offer a way for researchers to recognize what previously could not be known based on factual evidence, official

---

[5] Edweso was empty. The absence of the men felt like its own presence. Sometimes Akua would think that not much at all had changed, but then she would see the empty fields, the rotting yams, the wailing women. Akua's dreams were getting worse too. In them, the firewoman raged against the loss of her children. Sometimes she spoke to Akua, calling her, it seemed. She looked familiar, and Akua wanted to ask her questions. She wanted to know if the firewoman knew the white man who had been burned. If everyone touched by fire was a part of the same world. If she was being called. Instead, she didn't speak. She woke up screaming. (Gyasi, 2016, p. 186)

[6] Black holes grow as they collapse and absorb stars; the stars' energy disappears from the universe. Energy cannot be created or destroyed, supposedly. At least that's what they teach us in school, in Newtonian physics. But "laws" of the universe are not what we once thought they were. We aren't always taught complete truths, because truths transform.

accounts and data/archives, or direct observation (Cho, 2008; Crawley, 2018; Gómez-Barris & Gray, 2010; Gordon, 2008; D. Scott, 2008). By haunting, ghosts reject the primacy of empirical and official knowledge that perpetuate the state so that knowledge is not the point of research, transformation is.[7]

Ghosts haunt to change belief, though a person might not act as if this change is happening (*become brave*). Among many of us who work in and endure systems, our ghosts mostly go ignored (*or at least we pretend we can ignore them*). Ghosts trouble us researchers, who have been labeled experts despite what we cannot explain. What are our limitations in seeking a transformed world if we stand by technical and ontological modes of research (Derrida, 1994; D. Scott, 2008)? What kinds of truths do ghosts plant in our minds and hearts that cannot be covered up? What do we do with knowledge construction when knowledge isn't stable? (*If you can no longer pretend that absences are empty, then look behind the veil, sit with what's there, and follow changing realities toward what you will have become for freedom.*)

You'll have to trust yourself to understand ghosts, and you'll have to find your own way to this intuitive aspect of spirit- and soul-led research. As researchers, personally, we (Irene and Grace) attune to the tears that smudge our fieldnotes; the tickle of hairs rising on the backs of our necks as we walk into a classroom; the people we have never met, though we know their names and stories; the text messages with which research participants interrupt our nonresearch lives (*we interrupt the regularly scheduled programming of business as usual in institutions whose usual business is dehumanizing*).

> *Hauntings are processes of institutionalized, state-sanctioned violence. Ghosts use repetition in haunting. By haunting, ghosts change belief. Hauntings are processes of institutionalized, state-sanctioned violence. By haunting, ghosts change belief. Ghosts use repetition in haunting. Ghosts use repetition in haunting. Hauntings are processes of institutionalized, state-sanctioned violence. By haunting, ghosts change belief processes of institutionalized, state-sanctioned violence. Ghosts use repetition by haunting, ghosts change state-sanctioned belief. Hauntings are change processes of institutionalized violence by believing ghosts' repetition use. By haunting, ghosts change repetition of institutional violence processes.*

---

[7] When you are standing in the pulpit, you must sound as though you know what you're talking about. When you're writing, you're trying to find out something which you don't know. The whole language of writing for me is finding out what you don't want to know, what you don't want to find out. But something forces you to anyway. (Elgrably, 1984, para. 20)

The Somethings-To-Be-Done

If: "*The opposite, the endgame of opposing our dispossession is not possession—not haunting, though I'll do it if I have to; it is mattering*" *(Morrill et al., 2016, p. 5)*

Then: A purpose of hauntological research must be mattering (Love, 2019).

Being attuned to the tears, the tickles, the text messages is how we establish that the research participants matter, the researcher matters, the research relationship matters. Once attuned, how might a researcher heed the hauntings? Ghosts, according to Gordon (2008), are not simply returns to be celebrated or feared, to be nodded to and then set aside, but rather to be greeted. Ghosts must be treated with the dignity and respect they were unjustly denied. The aim, or "research objective," of ghostly conversation is not to distract the ghost from its desires, to luxuriate in being haunted, nor to persuade the ghost to tell you the something-to-be-done so that you can exorcise the ghost. The something-to-be-done is not a single incantation, and the somethings-to-be-done will never be comprehensive, nor pure, nor fixed (Shotwell, 2016). Each of us, complicit in oppressive systems, has interdependent somethings-to-be-done that together "[set] in place a different future" (Gordon, 2011, p. 66). The somethings-to-be-done have already begun, holding more rememories, more lifeways, more understanding.

With this spirit, we describe three transformative hauntological processes that construct mattering at interpersonal, collective, and societal levels: witnessing, rememorizing, and dreaming and transforming. When attesting to ghosts' mattering, "researchers" and "study participants" witness institutional violence inflicted interpersonally; feel and contribute to collective transformation through incomplete and heterogeneous rememories; and fuel the playful labor of dreaming and building otherwise.

Witnessing

Research question #1: Who (and what) are you bearing witness to (and for) through your research? When you witness, what claims are you making about who and what matters?

Witnessing is a spirit-led process of being haunted. It is receiving and often recording an account of injustice; it is to be with ghosts and feel traces of their pain, even though you cannot experience it directly. Heeding hauntings begins with witnessing: with being in relation with ghosts, with recognizing that ghosts are always horrifying but not always malevolent. Witnessing is how we affirm that the people in our studies matter, that their ghosts matter, that what has been erased matters. It is also how we know that *what* we are doing in the studies matters, *how* we are doing the studies matters, *our* presence in the academy matters—no matter the institutional violence that tells us we don't.

Witnessing calls forth response-ability to your ghosts as a researcher, to the ghosts of your "study participants," to institutional ghosts that haunt your research sites (Oliver, 2001). It requires holding a ghost's story in ways that re-member its complex personhood—not just its endurance of state-sanctioned violence—and savoring its survivance, its "active sense of presence over historical absence, deracination, and oblivion" (as cited in Patel, 2016, p. 9).[8] In this way, witnessing allows exchange and conversation—response.

Although witnessing attests—sometimes powerfully, sometimes transformatively—to who and what matters, witnessing alone cannot change the violence that produced the ghost, and could, in fact, reproduce it (Oliver, 2001). We are complicit in maintaining pasts as we witness them; we ask ghosts and targets of state-sanctioned violence to relive their pain, bringing it into presence. Research witnessing must toe a line through this dynamic of present violence rememories: because pasts become futures, rememories turn into the what-should-have-been and the something-to-be-done (Gordon, 2008; Whitlinger, 2020).

Rememorizing

> *Research question #2: What does your research forget, and does it do it on purpose? How does your research rememorize, and what does your research re-member? Can your research reconcile?*

A rememory is a story. Specifically, it is a story that helps us navigate the time when state-sanctioned violence is officially over and done, but the over and done stays (Gordon, 2008). Rememories are stories that were not written, could not be written, and should have been written: stories that build different worlds for more who's and what's that matter. Rememorizing makes it possible to do the work of release, re-membering, and reconciliation.

---

[8] The hand was tight on her left arm, before she turned and saw his face. He was pulling her up the street before she could utter a word. What the hell was this white man doing? People were watching but no one did anything, said anything. A colored woman could be grabbed on the street and no one said a damn word or uttered a peep. No matter where you went there was always some white man you had to tell to get his hands off you. When you least expected it, when you were lost in reverie about the good life in the city, these hands suddenly appeared, as if always waiting to snatch you. (Hartman, 2019, pp. 163–164)

These are not the same as forgetting:

> When we say, "Don't forget the milk," we indicate an act that should follow from the thought. It wouldn't do to say, "I was thinking about milk the whole time; I just didn't buy it." . . . Forgetting is a lack of action, not a lack of thought. (Hyde, 2019, p. 40)

Forgetting is an action of omission. Forgetting (the occurrence of state-sanctioned violence or the humanity of those to whom the violence is done) is what produces ghosts in the first place: "to forget victims is to victimise them twice" (Brewer, 2020, p. 38). Rather than forgetting or even forgiving, releasing the hold that memories have on us—so they no longer have power over us—is the first step in "putting the past back together again (re-membering)" (Wale et al., 2020, p. 16).[9] Re-membering takes the stories that ghosts need told in their quest for justice—memories that have been silenced or erased or foreclosed and never imagined—and elevates them alongside the stories that have been circulating.[10]

Reconciliation brings pasts we knew into conversation with pasts ghosts ask us to know through richly textured and heterogenous rememories. Reconciliation dances with, but is skeptical of, repair—which may not seem possible because much of what is lost cannot be restored, and because "enduring structural inequalities and injustices after conflict . . . keep the ghosts alive" (Brewer, 2020, p. 42). Reconciliation is not resignation; it is a collective process of rememorizing what has been, what could have been, and what must be (Whitlinger, 2020).

Ghosts haunt for a future neither—neither the past with changed dressings, nor something entirely unfamiliar. Not all ancestors or ghosts teach us how to rememorize, but the ones who do call for transgenerational rememorizing—for re-memberings, reconciliations, and reckonings that proliferate possibilities as opposed to a narrowly normalized past (Kumashiro, 2000). Rememorizing does not guarantee reconciliation and reckoning, but without rememorizing, we cannot dream or transform.

---

[9] "But is forgiveness that is coerced true forgiveness? asks Ona Friesen. And isn't the lie of pretending to forgive with words but not with one's heart a more grievous sin than to simply not forgive?" (Toews, 2019, p. 26).

[10] The album assembled here is an archive of the exorbitant, a dream book for existing otherwise. . . . The wild idea that animates this book is that young black women were radical thinkers who tirelessly imagined other ways to live and never failed to consider how the world might be otherwise. (Hartman, 2019, p. xv)

Dreaming and Transforming

> *Research question #3a: What does it mean to build alternative worlds where mattering matters? Will new worlds always have traces of this world? And whatever the answer, is that a problem and/or a solution?*

> *Research question #3b: What are your ghosts planting in your dreams?*

We'd like to write about building alternative worlds because that would seem to be the next step: material change committed to a belief system of personhood, worth, and success without capitalism, settler colonialism, racism. But change, too, can be ugly, unethical, or violent; and, as Lorde (1984) pointed out, "the master's tools will never dismantle the master's house" (p. 110). We also know that we can't leave our pasts behind. Heeding hauntings can be painful and exhausting; these structures are in our bones and in our land, not to mention in our brains.[11] The master's house is like a black hole, drawing everything to it with its force.

> It was written into the DNA of the Dream House, maybe even back when it was just a house, maybe even back when it was just Bloomington, Indiana, or the Northwest Territory, or just the still-uncolonized Miami Nation. . . . You wonder if, at any point in history, some creature scuttled over what would, eons later, be the living room, and cocked its head to the side to listen to the faintest of sounds: yelling, weeping. Ghosts of a future that hadn't happened yet. (Machado, 2019, p. 92)

But it turns out black holes may not be inescapable (Giddings, 2019; Hawking, 2015). Ghosts are like fugitive particles that manage to escape from black holes that are strong enough to consume universes; the particles tell us what to miss. Ghosts are knowledge transformed into energy that was never lost. If the future is always now (Campt, 2017), can we hold many paths to many mountaintops?

This is where we try to balance our dreams: those that truly make nonsense and are liberating for that reason, though they also respond to issues

---

[11] We know this from novels that imagine and rememorize family histories across multiple generations of colonization, slavery, and seeking repair: *Kindred*, by Octavia E. Butler (1979); *The Marrow Thieves*, by Cherie Dimaline (2017); The justice trilogy, beginning with *A Plague of Doves*, by Louise Erdrich (2008); *Homegoing*, by Yaa Gyasi (2016); *Pachinko*, by Min Jin Lee (2017); and, of course, *Beloved* (Morrison, 1987).

here in our world and time;[12] those that are almost possible, with individual and collective action; and those that are being lived out as "sweet, quiet spots of refuge" (Weis & Fine, 2012, p. 175).[13] Freedom dreams will never be realized without justice, reckoning, repair, release, and love (Kelley, 2002; Wale et al., 2020; Whitlinger, 2020). Significant pain and death have and will occur while futures are dreamt and razed. Yet dreams are not only arduous, grand visions; dreams are small moments of naming.

Transforming means taking steps to return, repair, and reckon with having no good options, and yet having all options. Building for ghosts makes way for ghosts to let go, so they are not trapped here with us. Maybe they are able to go because we've done the something-to-be-done. Or maybe they can stay to support and affirm and guide. What matters is that they can come and go as they wish rather than haunting out of desperation.[14]

---

[12] In their young adult fantasy novel, *Pet*, Akwaeke Emezi (2019) tackles this problem with the idea of what justice looks like in a world without the monsters of state-sanctioned oppression. In the city of Lucille, monsters that prompted violence and oppression have been eradicated, and systems remade. But adults are so wedded to their utopia that they cannot believe Jam (a transgender Black girl who speaks selectively and typically signs, which everyone in the city can also do, because inclusion) when she says that Pet has come to Lucille to hunt a monster. Jam is the only one whom Pet chooses to reveal itself to for quite a while, because no one else will believe.

[13] Committed to leaving no one behind, we rolled through the conference in a big, slow group of wheelchair users, cane users, and slow-moving people. Instead of the classic able-bodied conference experience most of us were used to, where able-bodied people walked at their able-bodied rate and didn't notice we were two blocks behind, or nowhere, we walked as slow as the slowest person and refused to abandon each other. People got out of the way. Instead of going out to inaccessible party sites, we chose to stay in, and ate and shared about our disabled lives. For some of us, it was our first time doing that. People cried, flirted, and fell in love.

CCA [Creating Collective Access] changed everyone who was present for it and a lot of people who just heard about it. It was just four days, but people went home to their communities transformed. We were no longer willing to accept isolation, or a tiny bit of access, or being surrounded by white disabled folks as the only kind of disability community we could access, or being forgotten. . . . Being part of that wild pack of slowness, talking tentatively about our disabled lives in ways we'd never said out loud before, changed everyone's lives. (Piepzna-Samarasinha, 2018, pp. 51–52)

[14] Visitation—Spirit Lights

I was standing at the sink washing the dishes and five or six, small bright lights appeared and spoke to me. They commented on what I was doing, washing the dishes. "Oh, it's good you are taking care of your family." They stayed for several days. If I made a cup of tea they would say, "That's good you are relaxing and taking care of yourself." They affirmed everything that I did, they told me I was good, I was doing good things. One day, after they had been visiting for nearly a week, I was talking to a friend on the phone and they let me know they were leaving, and before I could say goodbye they were gone. But everything had changed. I can't tell this story without crying. (Morrill et al., 2016, pp. 17–18)

Conclusion

As children, we (Irene and Grace) learned to greet guests and elders. When adults came to the house, we were expected to leave what we were doing to go to the door and greet the guests, smiling, bowing, and nodding as we awkwardly tolerated the ritual interactions of Asian American adults and children. When it was time to leave, we began another round of farewells with each family before we could depart. We could be wishing people goodbye for an hour or more. Every guest greeted every other guest, coming and going.

Now adults, we laugh over the memories these stories elicit. We talk about the cultural compasses that have encoded us to acknowledge and greet others, even amidst thoughts, work, kids, guests, phone, whatever—whenever we or they enter the room. Even on Zoom we do this. (Pause as Irene interrupts Grace mid-sentence to grin and wave at Grace's family.)

> Grace: It's formulaic and sincere. We greet someone by name when we come into a room, or we greet them so that they know we're in there, so we don't startle them. Even if you can't stop what you're doing, or if they're in the middle of something, you at least let them know that you're there and copresent. When you're a kid it's just a rule, but as you get older it becomes something more sincere.
>
> Irene: Yes, my family does the same. It feels—rude, maybe?—if someone comes into the room and doesn't say hello, like you wonder if they're mad at you. There's always an expectation to be ready to engage, which can be a lot sometimes; but also, how can you just not acknowledge that someone is there with you?
>
> Grace: You have to let them know that you know they're there.
>
> Irene: Maybe that's why ghosts haunt. It starts with their needing to know that we acknowledge them, that we know their names and stories. Not just their labels and traumas.

As researchers, we (Irene and Grace) try to reconcile the transformation of heeding hauntings with the histories of research and the construction of "knowledges" that attempt to dehumanize us as women of color (and Irene is disabled). This is why we have been haunted in our research experiences, by our silences, and by the institutional erasures we have participated in (Yoon, 2019). At the same time, greeting and heeding ghosts has healed (parts of some of) these lingering shadows, introducing us to love, wonder, and opportunities to be recognized and to recognize as complex and worthy persons (Chen, 2020). We matter, our research matters, and justice and dignity for Black, Indigenous, and persons of color—for queer persons, for disabled persons, for trans persons, for undocumented persons (literally absent from and tied to the structures of the nation-state), for all persons between space–time labels—our justice and dignity matter in schools as they do everywhere.

Some ghosts are warm; some are needy; some are heartbreakers. We are open to these and to visitations that challenge or scare us, because they matter, too. They ask us to strategically forget official accounts and rememorize the ones we witness. Heeding hauntings changes what we take as context, what claims we make, what we consider evidence, what becomes of our research, and therefore what we traditionally have been taught to value as the central purpose of inquiry. It changes how we greet and heed ghosts in the spaces and times we are in, the names and forces that we include in ritual acknowledgement and relation of copresence. As a research practice, heeding ghosts informs and transforms the something-to-be-done with the beauty, mundaneness, outrage, and mutability of complex persons with obscured pasts and phantasmagorical futures.

References

Brewer, J. (2020). Remembering forwards: Healing the hauntings of the past. In K. Wale, P. Gobodo-Madikizela, & J. Prager (Eds.), *Post-conflict hauntings: Transforming memories of historical trauma* (pp. 29–46). Palgrave MacMillan.

Butler, O. E. (1979). *Kindred*. Doubleday.

Campt, T. M. (2017). *Listening to images*. Duke University Press.

Chen, G. A. (2020). Bearing witness to mathematical ghosts: The ethics of teachers seeking justice. In A. I. Sacristán, J. C. Cortés-Zavala, & P. M. Ruiz-Arias (Eds.), *Mathematics education across cultures: Proceedings of the 42nd Meeting of the North American Chapter of the International Group for the Psychology of Mathematics Education* (pp. 525–529). https://doi.org/https:/doi.org/10.51272/pmena.42.2020

Cho, G. M. (2008). *Haunting the Korean diaspora: Shame, secrecy, and the forgotten war*. University of Minnesota Press.

Crawley, A. (2018). *Ghosts*. The New Inquiry. https://thenewinquiry.com/ghosts/

Derrida, J. (1994). *Specters of Marx: The state of the debt, the work of mourning, and the New International*. Routledge.

Dimaline, C. (2017). *The marrow thieves*. Cormorant Books.

Dolmage, J. T. (2018). *Disabled upon arrival: Eugenics, immigration, and the construction of race and disability*. The Ohio State University Press.

Elgrably, J. (1984). James Baldwin, the art of fiction, No. 78. *The Paris Review, 91.* https://www.theparisreview.org/interviews/2994/the-art-of-fiction-no-78-james-baldwin

Emezi, A. (2019). *Pet*. Make Me a World.

Erdrich, L. A. (2008). *The plague of doves*. HarperCollins.

Freud, S. (2003). The uncanny. In D. McLintock (Trans.), *The uncanny* (pp. 121–162). Penguin Classics.

Giddings, S. B. (2019). Escape from a black hole. *Scientific American, 321*(6), 50–57. https://doi.org/10.1038/scientificamerican1219-50.

Gill, M., & Erevelles, N. (2017). The absent presence of Elsie Lacks: Hauntings at the intersection of race, class, gender, and disability. *African American Review, 50*(2), 123–137. https://doi.org/10.1353/afa.2017.0017

Gómez-Barris, M., & Gray, H. (2010). Toward a sociology of the trace. In H. Gray & M. Gómez-Barris (Eds.), *Toward a sociology of the trace* (pp. 1–16). University of Minnesota Press.

Gordon, A. (2008). *Ghostly matters: Haunting and the sociological imagination* (2nd ed.). University of Minnesota Press.

Gordon, A. F. (2011). Some thoughts on haunting and futurity. *Borderlands, 10*(2), 1–21. https://link.gale.com/apps/doc/A276187005/AONE?u=anon~9470e14& sid=googleScholar&xid=9deaed34

Gyasi, Y. (2016). *Homegoing*. Vintage.

Hartman, S. (2008). Venus in two acts. *Small Axe, 12*(2), 1–14. https://doi .org/10.1215/-12-2-1

Hartman, S. (2019). *Wayward lives, beautiful experiments: Intimate histories of riotous Black girls, troublesome women, and queer radicals*. Norton.

Hawking, S. J. (2015, August 25.). *Hawking's comments on escaping black holes* [Video]. Lecture delivered at the 2015 Hawking Radiation conference in Stockholm, Sweden. https://www.youtube.com/watch?v=DkRDmJpthXg&feature=emb_logo

Hong, G. K. (2014). Ghosts of Camptown. *MELUS: Multi-ethnic literature of the United States, 39*(3), 49–67. https://doi.org/10.1093/melus/mlu025

Hyde, L. (2019). *A primer for forgetting: Getting past the past*. Farrar, Strauss and Giroux.

Kafer, A. (2013). *Feminist, queer, crip*. Indiana University Press.

Kelley, R. D. G. (2002). *Freedom dreams: The Black radical imagination*. Beacon.

Kumashiro, K. K. (2000). Toward a theory of anti-oppressive educa-tion. *Review of Educational Research, 70*(1), 25–53. https://doi.org/10 .3102/00346543070001025

Lee, M. J. (2017). *Pachinko*. Grand Central Publishing.

Lincoln, M., & Lincoln, B. (2015). Toward a critical hauntology: Bare afterlife and the ghosts of Ba Chúc. *Comparative Studies in Society and History, 57*(1), 191–220. https://doi.org/10.1017/S0010417514000644

Lorde, A. (1984). *Sister outsider*. Crossing Press.

Love, B. L. (2019). *We want to do more than survive: Abolitionist teaching and the pursuit of educational freedom*. Beacon.

Machado, C. M. (2019). *In the dream house*. Graywolf.

MacLure, M. (2013). Classification or wonder? Coding as an analytic practice in qualitative research. In R. Coleman & J. Ringrose (Eds.), *Deleuze and research methodologies* (pp. 164–183). Edinburgh University Press.

Morrill, A., Tuck, E., & Super Futures Haunt Collective. (2016). Before dispossession, or surviving it. *Liminalities: A Journal of Performance Studies, 12*(1), 1–20. https://www.proquest.com/docview/1787794449/citation/185B578E26164F73PQ/1?accountid=8360

Morrison, T. (1987). *Beloved.* Knopf.

Oliver, K. (2001). *Witnessing: Beyond recognition.* University of Minnesota Press.

Patel, L. (2016). *Decolonizing educational research: From ownership to answerability.* Routledge.

Perry, L. (1992). What's up? [Recorded by 4 Non Blondes]. Interscope.

Piepzna-Samarasinha, L. L. (2018). *Care work: Dreaming disability justice.* Arsenal Pulp.

Schwab, G. (2010). *Haunting legacies: Violent histories and transgenerational trauma.* Columbia University Press.

Scott, D. (2008). Introduction: On the archaeologies of Black memory. *Small Axe, 12*(1), v–xvi. https://muse.jhu.edu/article/241114

Scott, J. W. (1991). The evidence of experience. *Critical Inquiry, 17*(4), 773–797. https://doi.org/10.1086/448612

Shotwell, A. (2016). *Against purity: Living ethically in compromised times.* University of Minnesota Press.

Toews, M. (2019). *Women talking.* Bloomsbury.

Tuck, E., & Ree, C. (2013). A glossary of haunting. In S. H. Jones, T. E. Adams, & C. Ellis (Eds.), *Handbook of autoethnography* (pp. 639–658). Left Coast Press.

Wale, K., Gobodo-Madikizela, P., & Prager, J. (Eds.). (2020). *Post-conflict hauntings: Transforming memories of historical trauma.* Palgrave MacMillan.

Weis, L., & Fine, M. (2012). Critical bifocality and circuits of privilege: Expanding critical ethnographic theory and design. *Harvard Educational Review, 82*(2), 173–201. https://doi.org/10.17763/haer.82.2.v1jx34n441532242

Whitlinger, C. (2020). *Between remembrance and repair: Commemorating racial violence in Philadelphia, Mississippi.* The University of North Carolina Press.

Yoon, I. H. (2019). Hauntings of a Korean American woman researcher in the field. *International Journal of Qualitative Studies in Education, 32*(5), 447–464. https://doi.org/10.1080/09518398.2019.1597211

6

(RE)CONSIDERATIONS
OF ANSWERABILITY
THROUGH GIFTING

Christine A. Nelson (K'awaika/Diné) and Heather
J. Shotton (Wichita/Kiowa/Cheyenne)

When Amanda and Z invited us to contribute to this book and specifically explore how we maintain answerability in research, we started by questioning the notion of answerability through an Indigenous paradigm of collectivity and community. Previously, we wrote about how we (Chris and Heather) have engaged in Indigenous sisterhood/sister scholar practices while navigating the academy. We discussed how our collectivist values and communal practices while navigating the academy center a praxis informed by our individual and shared Indigeneity (Keene et al., 2017; Shotton et al., 2017). While this chapter is written by two of us, we want to ensure that we recognize our Indigenous sister scholars, who have been instrumental in helping us begin storying our experiences of being Indigenous scholars. Particularly, we build on our previous work with Indigenous scholars, Amanda R. Tachine, Robin Minthorn, and Stephanie Waterman, and our introduction of Indigenous scholar sisterhood practices (Shotton et al., 2017). In this chapter, we honor how collectivist values and communal practices shaped our meaning-making of answerability through gifting.

Answerability in research speaks to the onto-epistemological foundations of why and how research is realized and lived out (Patel, 2016). Through a broad discussion of what answerability means to us, we realized how the practice of gifting centered our commitment to remain answerable within academic spaces. Figure 6.1 serves as a reminder of how gifting centers collectivity and community to uphold our answerability to the communities

Figure 6.1. Indigenous sister scholars preparing cedar bundles.

Note. Sister scholar gifts (taken April 28, 2017; AERA; photo credit: Charlotte Davidson, Diné/Three Affiliated Tribes [Mandan, Hidatsa, & Arikara]).

we strive to support through our scholarship. Figure 6.1 shows us, a group of Indigenous sister scholars, reaching into a bag of cedar[1] to prepare bundles. These bundles were given as gifts to attendees at an academic conference presentation. The creation of the bundles, or gifts, served as a collective space to center our intentions with each other and to be mindful of the message we hoped to convey during our academic presentation, titled "Multiple Layers of Empowerment and Tension: Indigenous Research in Higher Education" (Tachine et al., 2017) at the 2017 Annual Meeting for the American Educational Research Association (AERA).

---

[1] Cedar is a plant relative that has significance for a number of tribes. While the origins and uses of cedar vary across tribes, it is generally used for blessings.

We share this image to emphasize that when preparing to share knowledge in academic spaces, we worry about more than rehearsing a PowerPoint slide and preparing talking points. Preparing gifts reminds us that research and scholarship, which is done in service to the community, happens when we collectively work together and intentionally create space to foster a shared understanding of the meaning of research and scholarship. With our community, we are able to center gifting as a conduit for remaining answerable to each other, to our colleagues, to our families and relatives, and broadly, our Indigenous communities. The gifting processes are tethered to intergenerational knowledge and are not always meant for public consumption. To be clear, the process of preparing gifts and the gift itself is a way for us to honor our teachings. It is not performative, meaning that gifting is not a transactional process where the gift is seen as a commodity (Kimmerer, 2013).

The purpose of this chapter is to explore how gifting helps answer the following questions about answerability:

- To whom do we answer when we engage with our research?
- To what and for what knowledge and teachings are we responsible?
- How do we engage in a praxis of answerability?

We understand these questions to be lifelong and intergenerational–generational ventures. While we begin with these questions, we do not assume one chapter can cover all—or even each—in full. Yet we strive to think big to see where our conversations collectively lead us to understand answerability in the research process.

In this chapter, we go beyond describing the practice of gifting and begin disentangling how gifting and answerability are conceptualized, honored, and lived out in academic spaces. We start by offering a cultural framing of gifting. Gifting is conceptualized as a collective and decolonial process that can begin to extend what answerability means in research. We identify the significance of gifting within Indigenous communities to help disrupt the notion of gifting from a capitalistic and financial wealth approach. We then share how we are connecting gifting to forms of answerability in the academy. This cultural framing further allows us to articulate how gifting creates a collective and healing space within the research process. Following this framing, through the process of Indigenous storying (Archibald, 2008), we begin to engage in intentional conversations with each other to learn about our teachings, past and present intentions, and the meaning-making of gifting. We learn how answerability that is tethered to gifting allows us to be innately connected to the research process. Through our process of Indigenous storying, we welcome a third author to our space. The third author is the Gift.

We acknowledge the animacy and intimacy of Gift. We honor the agency of Gift, as we see them acting as a third author to our process of storying. The Gift offers insight into how we challenge the capitalist nature of gifting and the tendencies for research to remain bureaucratic and distant as a transactional encounter. Gift then shares how gifting guides us in remaining answerable to the communities we are in relationship within our research. Gift emerged when we began disassembling the neoliberal machinery of academic research. We leaned into la paperson's (2017) notion of scyborging to see how Gift joined our conversation and became a living entity of change and answerability. We conclude by offering questions that need to be further considered when understanding the intersection of answerability and research.

Answerability and Gifting

Gifting in the academy speaks to how we maintain answerability to our community while operating in the liminal spaces of the academy. To better understand how we connect answerability with gifting, we offer a brief overview of how existing research frames answerability, then share how we are conceptualizing gifting as a form of answerability. A larger body of the existing research frames answerability as a theoretical concept to understand clinical and behavioral assessments (Miller, 2013; Shoemaker, 2015; Smith, 2015; Westlund, 2009). This body of research relates answerability to constructs of responsibility and morality at the individual level. Another body of research specifically addressed answerability related to research processes (Patel, 2014, 2016).

We align our work with understanding answerability in terms of the research process. Patel (2014) defines answerability as a framework of responsibility where individuals are stewards "of ideas and learning" (p. 371) throughout the research process. In the practice of stewarding knowledge through research, we understand that research carries intergenerational knowledge. To honor intergenerational knowledge we tend to pass on knowledge from ancestors to help future generations navigate and understand their journeys. We understand answerability as more than just considering one's ethical behavior in research. We push to consider answerability as an ontological consideration of how one's values help orient their lived responsibility to oneself and others (Shoemaker, 2015). It is important to note that the nuances of answerability have been explored by Indigenous scholars. However, answerability is often framed through constructs of respect, responsibility, reciprocity, and relevancy (Kirkness & Barnhardt, 1991) and not by using the word *answerability* per se. We attempt to strengthen how we connect answerability through an Indigenous paradigm to practices found within the academy.

We focus on the practice of gifting as a way to articulate and provide insight on how we live out answerability in the academy.

Gift is an interesting term that can be both a noun with many meanings as well as a verb. In management and economic studies, the research on gifting is reasonably substantial (see Davies et al., 2010). Management and economic research aim to discuss how gifting is a form of compensation or transaction that impacts how businesses operate and how those involved in the exchange interpret and reciprocate similar transactions. The values conversation on gifting is limited to unethical and coercive behavior. However, there is a distinct difference between the scope of previous research and what we aim to accomplish. We center gifting as a collective and decolonial research process underpinned by cultural teachings grounded in relationality (Wilson, 2008). From our Indigenous-centered approach, we draw on Anishinaabe scholar Robin Wall Kimmerer's (2013) words, "A gift creates ongoing relationship" (p. 26). This relationship is not just between the giver and the receiver. The relationship we have to and with the Gift is just as meaningful. Gifting opens up space for us to bring life to what answerability in the academy is. The Gift moves beyond compensation or transactional actions and can exist beyond physical items to include shared knowledge through time and story. The Gift in itself becomes a being, one who tethers us to other humans, two-, four-, six-, and eight-legged relatives, trees, plants, and even the perceived inanimate.

Through an intergenerational understanding, our process of answerability through gifting extends beyond our individual selves. Through our conversations, we developed a deeper understanding of how gifting embodies and strengthens the connections we have to our Indigenous academic relatives, our communities, our ancestors, and future generations. We connect our collective gifting story to the work of Kimmerer (2013) and her framing of gifts in Indigenous knowledge systems. Kimmerer helps us to understand gifts as relational, rooted in responsibility and reciprocity. Of this, she writes, "The essence of the gift is that it creates a set of relationships. The currency of a gift is, at its root, reciprocity" (p. 28). Gifts reaffirm our obligations to one another, and as our collective story reflects, the practice of gifting serves to remind us that we are all connected. In Indigenous teachings, there is a mutuality of duties and gifts (Kimmerer, 2013).

Process of Storying

Through Indigenous storying practices (Archibald, 2008), we provide personal accounts of how we engage with, speak to, and honor answerability through ancestral knowledge as we maneuver through methodological spaces. We engaged in two storying sessions and one follow-up session to recap the previous sessions. Each session lasted between 30 and 45 minutes. The storying sessions were loosely structured. We started the sessions with a broad topic to discuss but allowed the conversation to unfold organically. The first session focused on our earliest and most salient lessons of gifting. In the second session, we shared the teachings of gifting and how gifting keeps us answerable to our individual communities. Each session was a reciprocal and dialogical process, where one of us would begin and the other would listen, and then offer follow-up perspectives. We audio-recorded and transcribed the sessions, which allowed us to be present for each other's stories and to have a point of reference as we wrote.

Following the storying sessions, we continually revisited the audio and transcriptions because we understand that stories carry many lessons, and even our shared words could bring to light different meanings. In our third meeting, we recognized how session 2 built off session 1 but added more nuance to conceptualizing gifting. Our shared space of storying was beginning to bring together lessons and meaning-making that we did not have when we began.

Our first lesson was thinking about how we wanted to honor our stories as gifts. We began to appreciate our stories as a gift with animacy. Our storying gave us a moment to appreciate our time with each other and theorize how time, space, and immaterial can serve as gifts. We began to embrace our shared stories as gifts that

> come to you through no action of your own, free, having moved toward you without your beckoning. It is not a reward; you cannot earn it, or call it to you, or even deserve it. And yet it appears. Your only role is to be open-eyed and present. (Kimmerer, 2013, p. 24)

Seeing stories as gifts presented us with an opportunity to hold the sacredness of our relationship to each other and our relatives. Storying encouraged us to see our conversations as Gift, our third author. Gift, as a proper noun, honors their lessons and ability to shift and grow with us.

Recognizing the agency of Gift led us to our second lesson of how to honor storying. The modern practice of compartmentalization and categorization would not be appropriate for agency and knowledge shared by Gift. We wanted Gift to remain as whole as possible. We leaned into Lorde's (2017) notion of "poetry as illumination," where "it is through poetry that we give name to those ideas which are—until the poem—nameless and formless" (p. 1). We saw poetic transcription (Glesne, 1997) push the normative research boundaries of presenting transcripts. Glesne (1997) initially used poetic transcription to focus on one participant, but we adapted this approach to follow Wright and Balutski's (2013) approach of blending narratives across different participants. In this case, our stories are carefully and intentionally brought together to animate Gift.

Lessons From Gifts

We search our minds and hearts for memories, stories, lessons from Gifts

It was not called gifting in terms of a practice . . . though we were doing it

I always think of the feast days, the throws,

how as a kid it was a fun time to be part of that practice, but not really understanding or being told

What was the original purpose of it

This is the redistribution of wealth

Not material wealth or wealth as commodity, but a responsibility to the collective

Lessons from Gifts teach us that one of the worst things that you can be is stingy

Those first lessons come to us at different times, when we are ready to receive them

Gifts teach us in different ways

My heart remembers my Grandmother preparing us for a "giveaway"

I remember how meticulous she was about everything

"This is how we do it"

We give the best that we have

Always intentional about what we give

There was always a lesson in the practice about being generous

"When you give, it should be a sacrifice and that's because you want to give the best that you have"

Reminders to be intentional about what we're giving and how we're thinking about it

in a way that redistributes those blessings that we have

What they were giving to me were sacred blessings that they wanted to pass along

Gifting isn't about the material object, it's what the Gift embodies

If you have something and someone admires it then you're supposed to give it to them

There are expectations from those teachings

that important lesson of being generous

We gift things that are significant to us

Sharing something that is important or significant to you with someone else

It might be something that you already have, or you own, it might be something that someone's admired that you share with them

It involves love and care and generosity

When we give, we're giving with love and we're giving with intentionality

Whenever you're giving something very special to someone, it's also carrying whatever intentionality that it initially possessed

Gifts' blessings move forward

Gifts are not inanimate objects, we have spirit and life and lessons

Gifts have their own agency

Sometimes gifts speak to us, telling us when they're ready to be passed on to someone who really needs them

Gifting is not merely an act or a gesture. It's not to be engaged without care

Gifting is a process

It's a way that we embody teachings and beliefs

and Gifts connect us

Through these stories, Gift shares lessons with us that ground us in ancestral knowledge and orient our scholarly practices in academia. Much like the Grandmother teachings (Tachine, 2017) that our hearts remember, these instructions serve to guide us as we navigate our responsibilities and relationships as researchers. Next, we draw from the lessons of Gift to elaborate on two points.

"This Is How We Do It"

As we shared our lessons about, from, and with Gift, we returned to one of our grandmother's teachings about gifting, particularly within the context of a "giveaway,"[2] and her simple instructions of "this is how we do it." Embedded in those instructions of how we give, and the care taken in the process, were teachings about relationships and answerability. "Gifting isn't about the material object, it's what the Gift embodies." This focus on what gifting embodies disrupts the ontological framings of materiality and transaction and invites us to understand gifting through relationality. Gift reminds us that we are all connected, and the process of gifting honors our responsibilities to our relationships and fosters answerability in our scholarship. Gifting as answerability centers our research in relational ways (Wilson, 2008), reminding us that we are constantly in relationship with knowledge and thus have a responsibility to care for knowledge sharing. In our storying, we understood that there are multiple ways to articulate our expressions of answerability. Our Grandmothers' lessons remind us that practices may evolve over time, as do our relationships with teachings. When we enter academic spaces, we carry Gift's lessons with us, returning to instructions of "this is how we do it."

"Gifts Connect Us"

This collective story of lessons from gifts shared between Gift and us reflects our understanding of the teachings passed down to us, ancestral gifts of knowledge. We began this process by reflecting on our earliest remembered lessons about gifting. As we reflected on our own stories—sharing our first lessons, instructions from Elders and family, our relationships with gifts—as we began this process of remembering, we felt the presence of someone else in our conversation. Like a faint whisper reminding us another story was being told alongside ours, another voice to honor, Gift joined in. Kimmerer (2013) reminds us, "I could hand you a braid of sweetgrass, as thick and shining as the plait that hung down my grandmother's back. But it is not mine to give, nor yours to take. Wiingaask [sweetgrass] belongs to herself" (p. x). Kimmerer helped us to reflect on how we can honor our shared stories and lessons from Gift. "Gifting is not merely an act or a gesture. It's not to be engaged without care." Gifts have spirit and agency that connect us in different ways. It is within this framing that we honored Gift as a being, listened

---

[2] A giveaway is known by different names among various tribes (e.g., potlatch, special, giveaway, throws) and generally describes a process where families give away gifts to honor an individual, family, or a significant time.

to their stories, and began to braid them together with ours, bundling our lessons into a collective story of shared wisdom.

Gifts as Relationship

Gifts create and honor our bonds in different ways

A Gift isn't just a gift, it has life, it has spirit, it has teachings

Gifts connect us and uphold our responsibilities to one another

Maintaining our present-day connections with one another

tethered to ancestral knowledge

Always reminding us of our responsibilities to one another

Gifts carry a responsibility between the gift, giver, and recipient

solidifying that relationship

Gifting is a process that tends to our relationships

Asking the important questions of what is required of us to be in right relationship

Our relationships are reciprocal

Gifting and reciprocity and answerability

they're a process and an ongoing way that we seek to understand our place

a way that we seek to engage in our being

Intentionality

Humility

Are you doing it because you can or are you doing it because that's what's needed

There's a difference

What does land ask of us, what do the people ask of us, what do our ancestors ask of us

What do our relations require of us

We must constantly ask ourselves these questions

Stories are Gifts

Gifts from ancestors, both human and more than human

We carry stories and tend to them

revisiting them again and again

maintaining our relationship with the knowledge they hold

They come to us as Gifts

helping us to understand our connections

Gifts carry energy

Gifts carry our intentions

Constantly urging us to honor our relationships

And hold our responsibilities to them as sacred

Here, Gift continues to demonstrate and teach us that gifting is a paradigm that orients how we navigate the realities of research and academia. Much like original instructions shared through our tribal stories, "They are like a compass: they provide an orientation but not a map" (Kimmerer, 2013, p. 7). Like the previous section, we draw two points from Gift's works to help extend how we are conceptualizing gifting through answerability.

"Gifts Carry a Responsibility Between the Gift, Giver, and Recipient Solidifying That Relationship"

Gift shares their energy to show how we exist in relation with each other and the world and that responsibility to our relations should not be overlooked as academics. Gift shows us that our actions value relations. Our construction of knowledge through research is guided by Gift's emphasis on relations. As Patel (2016) states, "Answerability includes aspects of being responsible, accountable, and being part of an exchange" (p. 73). She continues to say that decolonial approaches to answerability help researchers understand "how their work speaks to, with, and against other entities" (p. 73). Gift extends answerability beyond existing definitions of who we are answerable to and teaches us that answerability is more than an ethical approach that primarily happens between humans. Gift help us dig deeper into our ontological understandings to foster a stronger understanding of our research process as Indigenous scholars and commitments to a decolonial praxis.

Additionally, Gift shares that gifting is connected to reciprocity and how collectively "they're a process and an ongoing way that we seek to understand our place . . . a way that we seek to engage in our being." In the spirit of imagining the unimaginable, we understand Gift helping us navigate and engage in decolonial praxis. Asserting Gift as our third author, colleague, and relative may sound misplaced when framed within Western research paradigms, but from a decolonial perspective, Gift pushes the ontological boundaries of how answerability and gifting disrupt the extractive nature of colonial research methods (Minthorn & Shotton, 2018). We recognize how Gift carries the knowledge of our ancestors and, in turn, speaks to the intimate and special relationship we have with them.

"Stories Are Gifts . . . Gifts From Ancestors, Both Human and More Than Human"

Through Gift's guidance, we understand how we can be more explicit in connecting research and answerability with more than human elements, like story, waterways, land, and animals. As of now, the recognition of elements as nonhuman elements continues to center the human. For example, society broadly accepts the notion that humans should not cause harm to the climate. The "do no harm" is framed from the perspective that climate change will make the world uninhabitable for humans. The call to be aware of how we are connected to climate is not for the sake of seeing climate as a relative. This is why we intentionally choose the (re)framing of elements as more than human. Beyond Indigenous ways of knowing, there is little conversation on how more than human elements as beings carry energy, life, and lessons (Deloria & Wildcat, 2001). "More than human" more accurately describes these relatives and honors their animacy. This energy and life are how we orient our answerability.

When we begin to acknowledge and honor Gift's existing animacy, we then understand the need for us to be clear and intentional with our practices. For example, the image showing us preparing cedar bundles offers one way we engage in gifting. What may be less evident is the importance and intentions of gifting cedar. While the tangible aspects of gifting a bundle of this sacred plant relative might be apparent, the gifting of cedar here requires more profound reflection. We turn to Diné scholar Charlotte Davidson (2018) to help us frame the learning relationship between humans and more than human beings:

> Indigenous learning modalities . . . or "beings" impart endless teachings regarding the manner of human existence . . . and incite a deeply felt engagement with the dimensions of learning because our human faculties are invited into an intrinsically communal learning process. (p. 40)

Additionally, gifting does not always have to be generated by a physical item. Gifting can come in many forms, and through Gift's teachings, we have a deeper respect for their teachings. Gift is teaching us how to be mindful of our actions. Just as our words will shift over time, we expect Gift to shift and grow.

Caring for Lessons

"Openings," as Glesne (1997) states, is a "clearing away of accustomed practices" and "releases a rare feeling of reflective play in interpretation and language" (p. 218). While Glesne is referencing the process of poetic transcription, we see openings as a way to extend how answerability through gifting is imagined and lived out in research. We began this storying process to grow into understanding and sharing how gifting transpires in our research process. We did not anticipate that we would be joined by a third voice along this process, that of Gift. Gift is here to teach us how to remain answerable to each other, the world around us, the ancestors, and future generations. Gifting is not a linear or transactional process. Instead, it is cyclical and creates, fosters, and sustains relations. As Gift has shown us, learning is a form of answerability. Who we learn for and from and what we learn guides more than just ethical practices or following research protocols. Learning is how we came to understand the intimate aspects of gifting. To continue Gift's teaching, we return to the questions that guided our entry into this conversation:

- To whom do we answer when we engage with our research?
- What knowledge and teachings are we responsible for and to?
- How do we engage in a praxis of answerability?

The lessons shared in this process guided us in new directions, reorienting our thinking and urging us to (re)imagine answerability and reflect on the possibilities of an otherwise in our research. Our reaffirmed relationships with Gift invited us to honor their spirit, listen intently, and care for their lessons.

Gift has taught us the importance of humility, care, and generosity. Through our storying, we invite other scholars to reflect on their own stories and connections to the stories we have shared. In much the same way that Gift demonstrated responsibility to our relationships through the generosity of their lessons, we want to share this gift with you as readers and fellow scholars. As an act of reciprocity, where we honor our mutual responsibilities to one another as we engage in knowledge sharing, we invite you to reflect with us on the following questions regarding answerability and gifting:

Answerability

- What is your relationship with answerability?
- Whom are you answerable?
- How might you bring life to what answerability in the academy can be?

Gifting

- What teachings from Gifts guide your research practices and praxis?
- How do Gifts connect you and uphold your responsibilities to others?
- How might you reimagine your relationship to and with gifting?

References

Archibald, J. A. (2008). *Indigenous storywork: Educating the heart, mind, body, and spirit*. UBC Press.

Davidson, C. (2018). The methodology of beauty. In R. S. Minthorn & S. J. Shotton (Eds.), *Reclaiming Indigenous research in higher education* (pp. 36–46). Rutgers University Press.

Davies, G., Whelan, S., Foley, A., & Walsh, M. (2010). Gifts and gifting. *International Journal of Management Reviews, 12*(4), 413–434. https://doi.org/10.1111/j.1468-2370.2009.00271.x

Deloria, V., Jr., & Wildcat, D. (2001). *Power and place: Indian education in America*. Fulcrum.

Glesne, C. (1997). That rare feeling: Re-presenting research through poetic transcription. *Qualitative Inquiry, 3*(2), 202–221. https://doi.org/10.1177/107780049700300204

Keene, A., Tachine, A. R., & Nelson, C. A. (2017). Braiding our (in)visibility: Native women navigating the doctoral process through social media. *Journal Committed to Social Change on Race and Ethnicity, 3*(1), 39–72. https://ncore.ou.edu/media/filer_public/f8/4b/f84bc3e4-8ce0-4f80-a341-a2fd601a12a2/keene_et_al___braiding_our_invisibility.pdf

Kimmerer, R. W. (2013). *Braiding sweetgrass: Indigenous wisdom, scientific knowledge, and the teachings of plants*. Milkweed Editions.

Kirkness, V. J., & Barnhardt, R. (1991). First Nations and higher education: The 4 R's—respect, relevance, reciprocity, and responsibility. *Journal of American Indian Education, 30*(3), 1–15. https://www.jstor.org/stable/24397980

la paperson. (2017). *A third university is possible*. University of Minnesota Press.

Lorde, A. (2017). *The master's tools will never dismantle the master's house*. Random House.

Miller, D. (2013). Answerability, blameworthiness, and history. *Philosophia, 42*, 469–486. https://doi.org/10.1007/s11406-013-9510-x

Minthorn, R. S. Z., & Shotton, S. J. (Eds.). (2018). *Reclaiming Indigenous research in higher education*. Rutgers University Press.

Patel, L. (2016). *Decolonizing educational research: From ownership to answerability*. Routledge.

Patel, L. L. (2014). Countering coloniality in educational research: From ownership to answerability. *Educational Studies, 50*(4), 357–377. https://doi.org/10.1080/00131946.2014.924942

Shoemaker, D. (2015). *Responsibility from the margins*. Oxford Scholarship Online. https://doi.org/10.1093/acprof:oso/9780198715672.001.0001

Shotton, H. J., Tachine, A. R., Nelson, C. A., Minthorn, R. Z., & Waterman, S. J. (2017). Living our research through Indigenous scholar sisterhood practices. *Qualitative Inquiry, 24*(9), 636–645. http://journals.sagepub.com/doi/pdf/10.1177/1077800417744578

Smith, A. M. (2015). Responsibility as answerability. *Inquiry, 58*(2), 99–126. https://doi.org/10.1080/0020174X.2015.986851

Tachine, A., Nelson, C., Shotton, H., Keene, A., Kaiwipuni, L., Davidson, C. E., & Youngbull, N. (2017, April 28). *Multiple layers of empowerment and tension: Indigenous research in higher education* [Conference session]. American Educational Research Association, San Antonio, TX. http://tinyurl.com/j86ffss

Tachine, A. R. (2017). Grandmothers' pedagogy: Lessons for supporting Native students' attendance at universities. In J. Frawley, S. Larkin, & J. A. Smith (Eds.), *Indigenous pathways, transitions and participation in higher education* (pp. 151–167). Springer.

Westlund, A. C. (2009). Rethinking relational autonomy. *Hypatia, 24*(4), 26–49. https://doi.org/10.1111/j.1527-2001.2009.01056.x

Wilson, S. (2008). *Research is ceremony: Indigenous research methods*. Fernwood.

Wright, E. K. A., & Balutski, B. J. N. (2013). The role of context, critical theory, and counter-narratives in understanding Pacific Islander indigeneity. In S. D. Museus, D. C. Maramba, & R. T. Teranishi (Eds.), *The misrepresented minority: New insights on Asian Americans and Pacific Islanders and the implications for higher education* (pp. 140–158). Stylus.

PART THREE

AFTER

7

BLACKLOVE STORIES

Keon M. McGuire, Kirsten T. Edwards, and T. Elon Dancy, II

The essay you are about to read is the result of Black Love. It is a creation of and a testament to Black kinship. Beginning as a series of communions among Black friends, the time spent crafting the idea was filled with laughter and comfort. We shared stories about how we've been loved, missed love, loved any(way) and otherwise. And from that space we weaved an essay textured by a Black-rooted existence in the world. BlackLove Stories is a love offering shaped collectively and insurgently, an indictment against imperialist individualism and toxic white culture camouflaged as "normal." Everything about this project and its completion has been Black life-giving, freedom labor. We hope you are able to receive it as a gift.

BlackLove[1] stories owe much of its form, substance, and existence to womanist/Black feminists love praxis and politics (Walker, 1983). In opposition to commercialized versions of (modern) love that are almost always tethered to capitalist profiteering, womanists and Black feminists have given us visions of love that are healing, restorative, and freeing (hooks, 2001). In a world that viciously works to negate Black women's humanity vis-à-vis technologies of subjugation that position Black women as always already objects of exploitation and someone else's desire, a Black feminist and womanist call to *begin* with Black women is a call to begin with those rendered most vulnerable to state violence, capitalist precarity,

---

[1] Our decision to join BlackLove, as such, in part reflects a digital literacy logic that announces a community anchored around and through an idea in pluralistic ways. In this chapter it is our attempt to mark the two terms as always in relation, one never away or beyond the other. It is to force a pause that invites readers to ask what happens as the surfaces of these ideas, histories, embodiments come against one another beyond the superficial. What might we imagine as the roots of these ideas, histories, embodiments intertwine, refusing to let the other go?

and existential erasure (Combahee River Collective, 1977/1982; Damned, 1973/1990).

It is through this incessant call that we are reminded that any politics and praxis of love must be foremost concerned with those whom the world says is undeserving of our love. Here, too, we must mark clearly the ways Black queer persons and collectives have offered us an expansive vision of what it means to love and struggle for the liberation of *all* Black people. The Combahee River Collective statement, an articulation of intersectional analysis and activism, emerged from a politics of collectivism that actively sought to dismantle the interlocking systems of "racial, sexual, heterosexual, and class oppression" (p. 13). Such an analysis is as much about clarifying a praxis of solidarity as it is a call by Black queer activists to extend race–gender critiques to explicitly engage (cis)heteropatriarchy (Johnson & Henderson, 2005).

Moreover, fundamental to a womanist/Black feminist episteme is a turn toward repair—a repair of how we see, understand, and live in relation with ourselves, others, the universe, the Orishas, the ancestors, and other-than-human beings. As Walker (1983) reminds us, a womanist "loves music. Loves dance. Loves the moon. Loves the Spirit. Loves love and food and roundness. Loves struggle. Loves the Folk. Loves herself. Regardless" (p. xii). To take up womanist/Black feminist love work is to continually center healing and make room for joy.

Perhaps most fundamentally, Black feminists and womanists' call to love forces us to ask, what is the true value of any struggle for freedom if we fail to consider the ways we exist in relation to ourselves and one another? To say we love ourselves and one another is to reject controlling images (Collins, 1990) given to us. It is to demand that we not internalize and reproduce the nation's commitment to physical, psychological, and spiritual violence in our relations with one another (May, 2016). It is to move toward a relationality predicated on a love politics of "mutual vulnerability" (Nash, 2019, p. 116). Here again, Black queer studies force us to confront how narrow notions of a race-gendered us disregard and dispose those who always already exist in excess (Johnson, 2001).

Yet, the question remains: what does any of this have to do with methodology? Nothing, if by methodology we mean the technocratic processes of research that are treated, in Dillard's (2012) prescient phrasing, as recipe. But if by methodology we mean a fundamental consideration for how we show up with/alongside others in human-to-human encounters, BlackLove is everything (Jackson et al., 2014). BlackLove means that the human being is placed above the demands of the research questions. BlackLove means holding spiritual and healing space for human beings to show up as their full selves with the sovereignty of their personhood honored. BlackLove means aspiring toward mutuality over and against hollowed notions of rapport. BlackLove holds at bay voyeuristic and fetishizing research demands. BlackLove means being prepared to help carry in one's body, spirit, and mind the joys, triumphs, burdens and traumas that we might ask other human beings to share with us.

In order to situate our own ways of thinking with/through BlackLove in/as methodology, we share three BlackLove stories. These stories explicate that which informs how we show up as Black scholars who do work with and alongside Black people. We conclude by pointing to possibilities of engaging BlackLove in methodology with and beyond what we have offered.

Kirsten: Self-Care and Black Women's Right to Love Ourselves

Caring for myself is not self-indulgence. It is self-preservation,
and that is an act of political warfare.

—Audre Lorde

The greatest spiritual lesson I have learned is self-love, which is remarkable considering the world doesn't provide Black women "self-love and care" roadmaps. It seems it's intent on convincing Black women and everyone around us that we're not worthy of love and care, even from ourselves. Instead, racist, gendered capitalism demands that Black women's value lie not in who we are as creations of God, but in what we can produce for others.

Racial capitalism (Robinson, 1983) warps everyone's sense of self, convincing us that individual worth is inextricably linked to wealth and production value. However, there's a particularly violent iteration reserved for Black women. The lie that we don't have a right to ourselves has been one of the hardest to shake, even among the most critical of us. The academy is particularly adept at reinforcing this lie with its hyper-surveillance and overburdening of Black women, its consistent engagement with us as domestic servants and property (Dancy et al., 2018).

As liberal middle-class whites began waking up to the ills of a culture of production and accumulation and its impact on the mind and body, the self-care industry exploded. And like anything that finds its way to whiteness and racial capitalism, it became corrupted. Self-care morphed into flagrant displays of consumption, reinforcing the very system that made the original intent necessary. This capitalist transformation obscured versions of self-care that relied on principles of self-love, inner reflection, and mindful solitude practiced in a variety of non-Western spiritual traditions. Most remarkable is the way self-care was bastardized and snatched away just as Black women began to access it.

The prohibition on Black women's access to healthy models of self-care became starkly clear to me a few years ago. I served on a conference panel, constructed by graduate students, that was focused on sustaining critical research agendas in an unjust academy. Pre- and post-tenure academics with various social identities comprised the panel. One of the panelists in particular is quite well known. She works in an area of racialized scholarship and has in many ways dominated that corner of the field. She's also a white woman, or should I say a white-bodied² woman. She's a white woman with a convenient genealogical relationship to a community of color. She's Rachel Jessica Dolezal-Krug with a few less lies (at least as far as we know). And like Dolezal-Krug, she uses her convenient genealogical relationship to enact anti-Blackness unconstrained. While Black, Indigenous, and people of color (BIPOC) regularly gather in hallway corners to whisper their annoyance with her, I have yet to witness someone check her publicly because (a) as critical scholars we seem to collectively struggle with recognizing practices of white supremacist power among those we've coded as not white, and (b) she's a superstar who wields a significant amount of power.

At the time I was in my 5th year, in the midst of preparing my dossier for submission. Suffice it to say, I was in an odd mental–emotional–spiritual place. On the cusp of the conclusion of a painful journey, I could smell the end! I think I was intoxicated from the scent, because I found myself engaging in unplanned Black radical honesty. I sat on several panels that year, advising graduate students on how to navigate an unjust academy. And I. Told. The. Truth. Everytime. The students responded eagerly, thirsty for transparency. The crux of my invocations remained: "Care for yourself because the academy will not!" I wanted them to take seriously the task of knowing and learning to heal themselves, learning how to conjure their own spiritual balm. I take seriously Alice Walker's (1983) appeal to separate periodically for health and healing, as well as Audre Lorde's (1988) demand that self-care is "self-preservation" and an act of "political warfare" (p. 332).

---

² I am deliberately using the term *white-bodied* here as opposed to the colloquial *white-presenting*. My choice is a linguistic effort to focus on the body and how the body functions as a material point of relationality that orients the world toward different people in particular ways (Ahmed, 2007). I'm also attempting to signal toward the way scholars use *white-presenting* to locate people who have cultural and political commitments to communities of color, but by "luck" of genetics appear white to the general population. In this way, the term "rescues" white-bodied people from critiques reserved for white people in critical spaces, a "no fault of their own" linguistic turn. When I say *white-bodied*, I'm trying to note how some people with a genealogical relationship to communities of color embody whiteness. I am attempting to demand an accounting for how people choose to live in white skin.

So while I shared, my heart was focused on Black women, and those of us who are repeatedly denied the right to ourselves. Those of us who are marked as servant and property, *for* others. In this panel I did the same thing, passionately shared my insights with vulnerability and bravery. And per usual, the graduate students responded with enthusiasm. I suppose Professor Dolezal-Krug was unused to not being the center of attention. As I spoke, she grew visibly irritated. (She also seemed unused to being near Black men. She sat fidgeting uncomfortably next to a brilliant, boisterous, Black male colleague, clutching her items like a white woman trapped in an elevator with a Black man [Yancy, 2012].) But that's for another essay.

Finally, with the targeted passive-aggressive precision only a seasoned white woman could exact, she interjected. She discredited all of my advice, specifically suggesting that self-care is Eurocentric and that based on her community's worldview the only kind of care people of color should participate in is "[collective] care." I was livid. I turned, looked her straight in her eyes, and gave her the deepest Hoodoo stare my Black Creole ancestors had given me. I damned her and her white ancestors to hell with my eyes and energy. But I didn't speak. Because although I was growing in bravery, I was still scared. I had not yet secured tenure, and she was the superstar scholar with professional power. To this day, I am ashamed of my choice, but it's the best I could do at the time. Another thing I'm learning to love myself through.

In the intervening years, I've had a lot of time to think about Professor Dolezal-Krug's anti-Black instincts that day. It really was one of the finest performances of whiteness I've ever witnessed! Let me explain. By positioning self-care as essentially Eurocentric she (a) performed a dominator move by switching the attention back to her and away from a Black woman's testimony; (b) undermined my (and by extension other Black women's) right to self-ownership and self-preservation; and (c) hoarded racial and moral authority, reasserting herself at the top of the "justice hierarchy" (Mills, 1997). Finally, insisting her comments emerged from her "community" served two additional purposes. First, it effectively protected her from critique by others who feared being perceived as discrediting "her community's" epistemic position. Second, it made "unvisible" (McKittrick, 2006) the long legacy of Black women's collective care praxes. To be quite clear, the academy's consciousness in regard to collective care is beholden to the intellectual and spiritual labor of Black women. Period. And if white women are going to deploy Black women's theorizations, they must be willing to engage those ideas in their fullest capacity. Dr. Dolezal-Krug was not.

Owing to her white-bodied-ness, she was unable to hear how I nuanced self-care from a womanist/Black feminist perspective. And most sadly, Black women students heard a powerful scholar remind them that they must be owned—if not by the academy, then by the community. They were told that it's an act of injustice for a Black woman to get quiet enough within herself to reflect deeply on her inner world, that they are not worthy of the simple luxury that is space and time. And by the far-reaching reverberations of systemic white violence, they were denied the opportunity to consider how taking the time for which they are worthy imbues them with the healing needed to serve their communities in love. This is what I'm most ashamed of, the fact that in that moment I didn't love myself enough to insist on their right to love themselves.

Keon: Luv Is My Inheritance: BlackLove as Humanizing Relationality

My grandmother, Christina McGuire, was born on February 11, 1945. My mother, Latanya McGuire Howard, was born on December 30, 1964. I, along with my identical twin brother Teon D. McGuire, was born on March 16, 1986. Being in her early 40s, grandmother was something Christina McGuire felt ill-fitting. It was from this moment of refusal and self-naming that Mama Luv was born. Though initially chosen as an affectionate name between grandsons and grandmother, soon to a broader community she became Mama Luv. In many ways, her name both captures and signals what I believe to be my greatest familial and community inheritance: a rich, textured, deep, abundant, and expansive BlackLove.

I grew up bearing witness to Black people who were grounded in a deep sense of dignity in their Blackness and humanness. Though white terror was always already present, we did not internalize white supremacy's failures as our own, such that it was only right Mama Luv would take brown shoe polish to darken Santa Claus's face on the door ornament during the holidays. Though certainly with its contradictions, I largely grew up in worlds where we fought to anchor our humanity in ways that were self- and collectively determined, that is to say sovereign.

I have come to understand this idea of sovereignty in at least two important ways as it relates to BlackLove. First, as the birth of Mama Luv's name represents, sovereignty emerges from an understanding that who I am to me/we is most important, particularly over and against denigrated tropes of Black people as sub/nonhuman and Black women as the "mule uh de world" (Hurston, 1937/2000, p. 14). It is a reminder that "you are your best thing, Seathe. You are" (Morrison, 1987/2004, p. 322). It is akin to hooks's (1990) discussion of radical Black subjectivity that starts at the point where resistance ends, finding resistance insufficient in the making of a whole self. A radical Black subjectivity opens up to possibilities because in this space/place one's personhood does not hinge on the colonizer's legitimacy or recognition.

Related, Quashie's (2012) notion of quietness has come to inform my understanding of sovereignty and its relation to BlackLove. Quashie argues that Black culture is too often axiomatically understood as expressiveness and political resistance that is public facing. Quashie proposes quiet as a way to ask what we might gain by giving up resistance as a place of departure for understanding Black culture. Through this narrative imposition of what it means to be Black, Black people are denied an interiority—something that is their/our own.

Both hooks (1990) and Quashie (2012), for me, open up the possibilities for a more centered, sustained concern for Black folks' relationality with/to one another that is not displaced by an *exclusive* concern with sociality. If sociality is a way to make sense of Black people's existence in a white supremacist world that attempts to overdetermine Black subjectivity from without (Gordon, 1995), then the concern becomes understanding Black people as always in response to the centrifugal force of white supremacy, settler colonialism, and heteropatriarchy (Dancy et al., 2018; Ferguson, 2004). Instead, relationality asks, in spite of this arrangement, how do you treat Black (and other structurally vulnerable) people as the measuring stick for the quality of human you are? How generous are you with what you have? Do you side with the powerful over and against those most vulnerable at your benefit and their expense? Do you lead with true humility? It was through an embodied and storied BlackLove that I learned how to be in the world and the legacy I was expected to carry on.

Growing up with the privilege of living in a multigenerational household, and the gift of spending time with many elders—including my great-great-grandmother Josephine Canty who transitioned on February 1, 2000 at the age 102—I was immersed in rich oral histories. I learned how my maternal great-grandmother, Rosa B. Stokes, aka Smiley—who transitioned on April 28, 2006 at the age of 88—used her spacious two-story home to raise children not her own and how my great-grandfather, James Stokes, would routinely bring extra bread home from the bakery to share with the folks in the neighborhood. It was Mama Luv who stewarded these stories in such a way that highlighted the best while vigorously defending against even the slightest of detractions. She knew then, what I know now: Our lives are carried on by those who share our stories, and we, Black people, are worthy of the most humanizing and most glorious stories in all their contradictions.

Still, it was my family's *living* that impressed most upon me what it meant to aspire toward the best of BlackLove. Mama Luv shared with prideful responsibility the story of getting a good, union job at a fiber optics factory and immediately going back to help her two girlfriends study for and pass the entrance exam. It was her insistence that if we were with our friends and we ordered fast food, everyone had to split the meal evenly. It was also my mother's and father's (Derrick Howard) example of helping a neighbor pay their light bill, even when we did not have. It was their example of delivering meals on wheels, even when, as my mother would say, she doesn't know the last time she filled her gas tank all the way up.

These moments of BlackLove—or examples of true love for Black people—made clear that BlackLove at its best is a verb. BlackLove requires that we demand, not request, the sovereign territory of a dignified personhood. BlackLove abhors hoarding and embraces generosity. BlackLove knows that not everything we know is to be known by *everyone*.

Elon: Black Male Educational Studies,[3] Black Feminisms, and the Loud Silence: Can We Talk?

> Love takes off the masks that we fear we cannot live without and know we cannot live within. I use the word "love" here not merely in the personal sense but as a state of being, or a state of grace—not in the infantile American sense of being made happy but in the tough and universal sense of quest and daring and growth.
>
> —Baldwin (1963/1992, p. 95)

I write this essay as the U.S. empire announces Joe Biden is its next president following days of vote tabulation processes, speculative media outcomes, and fraudulent Donald Trump tweets. Following media projections of a contest winner, a telling social media debate emerged about Black voting patterns, particularly Trump's gain in Black voters and the gender differences in these gains. While Black people mostly voted for Biden (compared to all other racialized groups), nearly 20% of Black men voted for Trump compared to nearly 10% of Black women. Confronting this data, many saw this as an opportunity for gender analysis to interrogate this difference. In the exchange, some dialoguers added an important caution: If Trump wins reelection, this Black gender difference could not singularly explain the win, and any attempt to overrepresent Black men's votes participated in a form of white supremacist profiling. I also witnessed others, mostly Black men, accuse those with a gender critique as participating in their own white supremacist "divide and conquer" strategy that disallows Black men to think and vote differently from a Black majority. I did not agree with this,

---

[3] Throughout this section, the use of "Black male educational studies" or "Black male studies" is rooted in a Black studies grammar that references a subfield of educational studies almost exclusively based on the experiences of Black cisgender men. In part, because of its assumed coupling of sex/gender, "Black male educational studies" has pushed out the work of Black feminist and queer of color theorizing. As such, the use of *male* here does not reflect a commitment to a biologically anchored notion of gender, but rather reflects an area of study that we hold up for critique.

as the argument ignored gender as a set of power relations. It is this kind of obstruction—a refusal to examine patriarchy—that inspires my writing here. The social media exchanges remind me, an education scholar, of analogues within educational research. To be sure, while much of my writing here implicates educational research more broadly, I focus my reflection on Black male educational studies and bear witness to the erasure of Black feminist theorizing in gender-based research designs as barrier to Black academic solidarities. I argue that Black male educational studies matter within BlackLove politics but call for, in the words of Baldwin (1963/1992), "quest and daring and growth" (p. 95).

A cornerstone in Black feminist research, the Combahee River Collective (1977/1982) statement recalls Black feminist challenges with Black men: "We struggle together with Black men against racism, while we also struggle with Black men about sexism" (p. 16). For nearly 15 years, I have conducted research studies on formalized education settings as sites of power and hegemony, with particular questions about the ways Black boys and men simultaneously occupy spaces of racialized powerlessness and gendered power. Unsurprisingly, I read countless studies about Black boys and men and chair several doctoral student dissertations on their experiences. Across a near supermajority of these studies, I notice a pattern: Many articulate a racialized significance but ignore a gendered one, although all the study participants are men-identified. Black feminisms have long provided language for the troubling impacts of this academic phenomena—namely, in contexts of patriarchy, all the Blacks become men (Hull et al., 1982). However, the evidence is often illogical, selective, inaccurate, and decontextualized (Crenshaw, 2014). One outcome is a coterminous relation in which Black people's experiences and desires must reflect Black men's experiences and desires, and research contextualized within patriarchy is largely the domain of scholarship on Black girls, women, and queer people. The ways cis-heteropatriarchy shapes Black boys' and men's educational experiences remains understudied, yet Black male studies, even those that assume the cis-heterosexuality of Black boys and men do so without a necessary gender analysis. This is a loud silence.

Motivated by Baldwin's (1963/1992) notion of love as growth, I call forth lessons learned from readings of several Black boys' and men's lives, including my own. First, Black feminist intellectual thought is urgent to how we understand Black boys and men's experiences in U.S. schools, colleges, and society, and, perhaps more importantly, mapping freedom from them. However, much of the research on these populations is uncomplicated around gender (unless explicitly asking about it) in various aspects of research design including study significance, theoretical framework, and researcher positionality, among other elements. Further, the unwillingness of researchers to frame their foci in relation to white supremacy and patriarchy perpetuates a longtime injustice toward Black feminist scholarship—particularly that Black feminist scholarship is only useful for understanding Black girls and women's experiences. However, Black feminist theory informs, nuances, and expands our thinking about everyone's humanity (or banishment from it): The analytic potential of intersectionality, for instance, which requires confronting domination in matrix (Collins, 2008), has been underdeveloped in studies of Black boys and men and, in turn, has restricted how we study this population in educational contexts.

As I have argued elsewhere (Dancy, 2013), two fundamental tendencies in the literature shape methodological and theoretical limitations: the reluctance of researchers to explore fully how the analytic strength of gender and intersectionality can inform the knowledge base on Black boys and men. The traditional schematic power of race continues to destabilize the importance of intersectionality, namely the inclusion of patriarchy as a social organizer in how Black boys are socialized and socialize. To the extent that we study only Black boys and men without a patriarchal analysis, we do the work of exceptionality, which concurrently ex-communicates Black girls and women from Blackness. Black feminisms offer an urgent intervention here, as this scholarship requires an engagement of Black boys as both raced and gendered beings at the same time. As a teacher, advisor, discussant, and editor, among other roles, I require Black male studies to engage with Black feminist thought to dissuade any suspicion that anti-Blackness only shows up as the sambo and the beast, lest we forget the mammy, the jezebel, and the sapphire. Yet, all too often, much scholarship on Black men falls into this trap. The research designs must make an intersectional case, not an exceptional one.

The second tendency, if it remains unclear, white patriarchy (like the kind in the West) is an anti-Black affair. In other words, discursive shifts that assume "all the Blacks are men" uplift systems of white supremacy simultaneously. While some Black radical tradition scholars argue that anti-Blackness constitutes a structure that evicts Black people from humanity altogether and therefore gender, the qualitative differences produced for Black people still reveal aspirations and participation within white systems of power (Spillers, 2003). Hence, the plethora of Black male studies that fail to contextualize gender-based research designs within critical gender analysis actually facilitate the work of white patriarchy. Crenshaw (2014) called our attention to this in a critique of Barack Obama's My Brother's Keeper Initiative when she opined, "Perhaps the exclusion of women and girls is the price to be paid for any race-focused initiative in this era" (para. 4). To be sure, this discussion does not call for the elimination of Black male studies; on the contrary, it calls for the more rigorous theorization of Black men, a theorization that simultaneously assumes that more than Black men are Black and that Black men are not all cisgender and heterosexual. A guiding question for research framing emerges: While a study may include Black cisgender boys and men only, how does the research design implicate Black girls, women, queer, and gender nonconforming persons?

Taking seriously bell hooks's (1994) observations about education as a practice of freedom, I offer that researching for freedom is designing studies on Black boys and men in a way that assumes Black girls, women, and Black people who are neither need to get free, too. I worry that the uncritical exclusion of Black feminist theorizing from studies of Black boys and men participates in the white patriarchal empire's operations to prevent Black women from reproducing themselves. While on the one hand we can point to studies suggesting the dismissal of Black women and Black feminist scholarship (Edwards & Baszile, 2016), we can point to acts of forced sterilization of Black women's bodies on the other. Both are sites that refuse Black women's reproduction, and my fear is that the research on Black boys and men participates in such a project, sterilizing the intellectual wombs of Black women feminists. Research as practices of freedom and love would therefore require responding to this reality as a reproductive justice intervention.

BlackLove and Methodology

Black scholars have long critiqued how our ways of being and knowing are devalued and discarded within academic institutions. As Black queer studies remind us, Black people—figured as deviant, nonheteronormative vis-à-vis gender and sexual heterogeneity (Ferguson, 2004)—can serve as the raw, exploitable material for serious theory and scholarship, but never originator or author—that is, always object, never subject. Our BlackLove stories take up Black onto-epistemology from a place that accepts our humanity and works against the mere praxis of translation (Boveda & Bhattacharya, 2019; McGuire & Cisneros, 2020). Our stories elevate the centrality of relationality within BlackLove and evidence BlackLove's insistence on sincere solidarity, relationships that cultivate space to "see" and "hear" one another for mutual edification, resisting ego-driven, violent interactions. Our stories also connect to the African-centered practice of pedagogical storytelling, our ancestral legacy. Black elders for generations have crafted stories to impart spiritual lessons, map the fugitive path to freedom, and insist on our humanity. Storytelling is fertile soil and a portal to loving communication.

From an onto-epistemological place of BlackLove, a consideration for relationality makes clear not only what is necessary and possible, but also what is at stake within the context of (re)search among and alongside Black people. Though often—yet, uncritically—cast off as self-indulgence, Black scholars must wrestle foremost with a relationality to one's self in any methodological experience. If white supremacy, cis-heteropatriarchy, the afterlife of slavery, and settler colonialism (Dancy et al., 2018) are predicated upon a violent alienation of Black diasporic people from themselves/their communities, then BlackLove is a healing balm through which we might repair and find wholeness. Particularly for Black women and Black queer folks, Lorde (1988) makes clear that caring for one's self is a radical act of love and serves as the basis for self-definition.

A consideration for relationality is also about ensuring we show up in *right relations* with others. Through our stories we speak to the ways BlackLove guides us toward a deep concern for those whom we enter this experience of (re)search with. We seek to understand in what ways we are available to serve, holding spiritual and emotional space for those whom we colabor with. Aware of the ways Western onto-epistemological norms of research often lead to extraction, a methodology that thinks with/alongside BlackLove remains suspicious, always interrogating ways one might slip into complicity with such priorities. This is not to say there is some pure space from which one can sit within the academy and do this work, but it is to say that one might find ways of refusal and resistance in the questions we ask, the relationships we build, and what we share with the world.

Relatedly, communicating the truths embedded in these Black dialectical tensions for African-descended communities happens in the context of stories (Ani, 1994; Lincoln & Mamiya, 1990). Indeed, storytelling is an African retention (Carney, 2001; Gomez, 1998). The power of orality for Black learning is poignantly seen in the loving pedagogical practices of Black women writers, or what Edwards and Baszile (2016) describe as "scholarly rearing" (p. 87). Drawing on Black communal logics, Black women writers have employed testimony, storytelling, and other forms of counternarrative to *talk back* (hooks, 1989) to intersecting systems of power (Cannon, 1995; Collins, 1990; Crenshaw, 1990; Dillard, 2012; Edwards, 2014; Lorde, 1984). Their love storying has excavated the nuances embedded in powered relationality while simultaneously providing hope for a free Black future. The present essay draws on this womanist/Black feminist legacy. Our stories, individually and collectively, decenter traditional white, masculine ways of knowing. Through testimonial storytelling we apply an African-centered lens to interpret our lives and experiences as Black scholars.

We, too, invite readers to think with and beyond what we have not taken up here. How might BlackLove offer our methodological praxis more expansive visions of freedom, healing, joy? How might we understand BlackLove as a project of *sincere* solidarity across/between racial communities? What might it mean to think of BlackLove in relation to/with land, waterways, and time through African cosmologies (e.g., Orishas) that understand human/other-than-human and then/now as not-so-discrete existences? How might we sit with BlackLove and "collective healing . . . as we remember in ways that move us to action [with] our agrarian past" and "in relation to the body that is the earth and the body that is our flesh" (hooks, 2009, p. 47)?

Our goal here is not to essentialize Blackness, Black people, or BlackLove. From our own locations and within our individual histories, we share stories of how BlackLove grounds us first as human beings and subsequently as researchers. We share these stories as an invitation for readers to think how BlackLove might animate, orient, and anchor their work with Black people and communities.

References

Ahmed, S. (2007). A phenomenology of Whiteness. *Feminist Theory, 8*(2), 149–168. https://doi.org/10.1177/1464700107078139

Ani, M. (1994). *Yurugu: An Afrikan-centered critique of European cultural thought and behavior.* Nkonimfo.

Baldwin, J. (1992). *The fire next time.* Vintage Books. (Original work published in 1963)

Boveda, M., & Bhattacharya, K. (2019). Love as de/colonial onto-epistemology: A post-oppositional approach to contextualized research ethics. *Urban Review, 51*(1), 5–25. https://doi.org/10.1007/s11256-018-00493-z

Cannon, K. G. (1995). *Katie's canon: Womanism and the soul of the Black community.* Continuum.

Carney, J. A. (2001). *Black rice: The African origins of rice cultivation in the Americas.* Harvard University Press.

Collins, P. H. (1990). *Black feminist thought: Knowledge, consciousness, and the politics of empowerment.* Unwin Hyman.

Combahee River Collective. (1982). A Black feminist statement. In G. Hull, P. B. Scott, & B. Smith (Eds.), *All the women are White, all the Blacks are men, but some of us are brave: Black women's studies* (pp. 13–22). Feminist Press at City University of New York. (Original work published in 1977)

Crenshaw, K. (1990). Mapping the margins: Intersectionality, identity politics, and violence against women of color. *Stanford Law Review, 43*(6), 1241–1299. https://doi.org/10.2307/1229039

Crenshaw, K. (2014, July 29). The girls Obama forgot. *The New York Times*. https://www.nytimes.com/2014/07/30/opinion/Kimberl-Williams-Crenshaw-My-Brothers-Keeper-Ignores-Young-Black-Women.html

Damned. (1990). *Lessons from the damned: Class struggle in the Black community* (2nd ed.). Times Change Press. (Original work published in 1973)

Dancy, T. E., II. (2013). (Un)doing homogeneity in qualitative research: Exploring manhood among African American male collegians. In T. L. Strayhorn (Ed.), *Living at the intersections: Social identities and Black collegians* (pp. 153–169). Information Age.

Dancy, T. E., II, Edwards, K. T., & Earl Davis, J. (2018). Historically White universities and plantation politics: Anti-Blackness and higher education in the Black Lives Matter era. *Urban Education, 53*(2), 176–195. https://doi.org/10.1177/0042085918754328

Dillard, C. (2012). *Learning to (re)member the things we've learned to forget*. Peter Lang.

Edwards, K. T. (2014). Teach with me: The promise of a raced politic for social justice in college classrooms. *Journal of Critical Thought and Praxis, 2*(2), 1–20.

Edwards, K. T., & Baszile, D. T. (2016). Scholarly rearing in three acts: Black women's testimonial scholarship and the cultivation of radical Black female inter-subjectivity. *Knowledge Cultures, 4*(1), 85–99.

Ferguson, R. A. (2004). *Aberrations in Black: Toward a queer of color critique*. University of Minnesota Press.

Gomez, M. A. (1998). *Exchanging our country marks: The transformation of African identities in the colonial and antebellum South*. The University of North Carolina Press.

Gordon, L. R. (1995). *Fanon and the crisis of European man: An essay on philosophy and the human sciences*. Routledge.

hooks, b. (1989). *Talking back: Thinking feminist, thinking Black*. South End Press.

hooks, b. (1990). *Yearning: Race, gender, and cultural politics*. South End Press.

hooks, b. (1994). *Teaching to transgress*. Routledge.

hooks, b. (2001). *All about love: New visions*. Harper Perennial.

hooks, b. (2009). *Belonging: A culture of place*. Routledge.

Hull, G. T., Bell-Scott, P., & Smith, B. (Eds.). (1982). *All the women are White, all the Blacks are men, but some of us are brave: Black women's studies*. Feminist Press at City University of New York.

Hurston, Z. (2000). *Their eyes were watching God*. HarperCollins. (Original work published in 1973)

Jackson, I., Sealey-Ruiz, Y., & Watson, W. (2014). Reciprocal love: Mentoring Black and Latino males through an ethos of caring. *Journal of Urban Education, 49*(4), 1–24. https://doi.org/10.1177/0042085913519336

Johnson, E. P. (2001). "Quare" studies, or (almost) everything I know about queer studies I learned from my grandmother. *Text and Performance Quarterly, 21*(1), 1–25. https://doi.org/10.1080/10462930128119

Johnson, E. P., & Henderson, M. G. (2005). *Black queer studies: A critical anthology.* Duke University Press.

Lincoln, C. E., & Mamiya, L. (1990). *The Black church in the African American experience.* Duke University Press.

Lorde, A. (1984). *Sister outsider.* Crossing Press.

Lorde, A. (1988). *A burst of light: Essays.* Firebrand Books.

May, V. M. (2016). Anna Julia Cooper's Black feminist love-politics. *Hypatia, 32*(1), 35–53. https://doi.org/10.1111/hypa.12275

McGuire, K. M., & Cisneros, J. (2020). Against unseeing: Choosing an embodied ethics of disidentification. *Qualitative Inquiry, 26*(8–9), 1079–1089. https://doi .org/10.1177/1077800419881663

McKittrick, K. (2006). *Demonic grounds: Black women and the cartographies of struggle.* University of Minnesota Press.

Mills, C. W. (1997). *The racial contract.* Cornell University Press.

Morrison, T. (2004). *Beloved.* Random House. (Original work published in 1987)

Nash, J. C. (2019). *Black feminism reimagined: After intersectionality.* Duke University Press.

Quashie, K. (2012). *The sovereignty of quiet: Beyond resistance in Black culture.* Rutgers University Press.

Robinson, C. J. (1983). *Black Marxism.* The University of North Carolina Press.

Spillers, H. J. (2003). *Black, white, and in color: Essays on American literature and culture.* The University of Chicago Press.

Walker, A. (1983). *In search of our mothers' gardens: Womanist prose.* Harcourt Brace.

Yancy, G. (2012). *Look, a White! Philosophical essays on Whiteness.* Temple University Press.

8

LEARNING FROM ABOLITION

Reconsidering the Carceral in Educational Research Methodologies

Kyle Halle-Erby and Harper Keenan

I wake up & it breaks my heart. I draw the blinds & the thrill of rain breaks my heart. I go outside. I ride the train, walk among the buildings, men in Monday suits. The flight of doves, the city of tents beneath the underpass, the huddled mass, old women hawking roses, & children all of them, break my heart. There's a dream I have in which I love the world. I run from end to end like fingers through her hair. There are no borders, only wind. Like you, I was born. Like you, I was raised in the institution of dreaming. Hand on my heart. Hand on my stupid heart.

—Awkward-Rich (2020, para. 1)

W e write this chapter in the midst of (another) global catastrophe. The COVID-19 pandemic has ravaged communities across the world. As many scholars and artists have commented, the pandemic has seemed to reveal or deepen a wide range of social problems, from the rise of global fascism to anti-Black police violence, to expanding income inequality, to climate devastation. We struggle with feelings of powerlessness in the face of these compounding crises. As educational researchers, we play a role in shaping how young people and their educators might work together to imagine and build different futures. Such work requires a deep examination of the roots of social harm coupled with careful analysis of how to address those harms directly without throwing people away. This reveals a conceptual convergence between the contemporary prison abolition movement and educational research.

Although the idea of eradicating the prison may seem impossible to many, asking ourselves what we would do differently if we sought to eliminate incarceration as a solution to social problems enables a necessary paradigm shift for those who work in education. Although abolition demands elimination (of the prison, of the police), it is ultimately about *building* new ways of living together. Prison abolition invites a relational praxis of collective freedom and care. It seeks an alternative to the ways that capitalism often encourages us to turn away from each other in order to do our jobs, to make enough money to eat, to stay housed, or to otherwise meet our needs. To us, Awkward-Rich's poem speaks to the ways so many of us still recognize the world we are not necessarily meant to see—a window of possibility. Abolition asks us to exist in closer relationship to one another. As Black trans feminist Marquis Bey (2020) writes, this relation requires a kind of "mutuality in which one can care for and share affinity for others without needing to possess them" (p. 45). Abolition is driven by knowledge produced within the conditions of unfreedom imposed by colonial societies: enslavement, incarceration, trusteeship, and psycho-medical institutionalization among them. Due in part to the very structures that abolition seeks to eradicate, much of that knowledge has never been formally recorded. Abolition, in scholarship and in practice, does not belong to any one person. Instead, it is a shared dream of survival not yet realized. The dreams of the unfree and the enslaved have been forcefully erased from widespread public consciousness, yet they surround us at the same time. As Angela Davis (2003), one of the founding leaders of the contemporary abolition movement, has argued, this "simultaneous presence and absence" is purposeful design:

> We take prisons for granted but are often afraid to face the realities they produce. After all, no one wants to go to prison. Because it would be too agonizing to cope with the possibility that anyone, including ourselves, could become a prisoner, we tend to think of the prison as disconnected from our lives. (p. 15)

The designed obfuscation of unfreedom shapes all aspects of abolitionist study. We start from the premise that our study of abolition will fail to adequately engage the knowledge of the unfree. Saidiya Hartman (2008) describes a similar struggle in writing histories of enslavement:

> The task of writing the impossible . . . has as its prerequisites the embrace of likely failure and the readiness to accept the ongoing, unfinished and provisional character of this effort, particularly when the arrangements of power occlude the very object that we desire to rescue. (p. 10)

Through Hartman, we interpret abolition as praxis built in motion, on the way to an unknown horizon. As scholars, we are accustomed to reading in order to develop our own knowledge. In studying abolition, we read knowing that reading is never enough; this may be the first lesson of abolition. Trans scholar-activist Leslie Feinberg (1998) reminds us that "for revolutionaries, theory that is not a guide to action is a worthless intellectual exercise. Our analysis has to be as taut as a diving board that enables us to springboard into the fray" (p. 115). As a practice-driven field, educational research offers opportunities for praxis. For abolitionists, education can provide a way to practice new ways of learning and relating to one another that are not rooted in systems of discipline. At the same time, the history of educational research is bound up within carceral networks. In this chapter, we begin with a brief introduction to the relationship between prison, schooling, and education. Then, drawing on foundational texts in the study of abolition, we explore how abolition might inform educational research. We conclude by sharing our current commitments as students of abolition in our work.

Prison Abolition and the School: A Brief History

The origins of the contemporary fight for prison abolition are traceable to the global anti-slavery movement, connected within consistent but changing structures of unfreedom. In the United States, prisons are viewed by many abolitionists as a part of the "afterlife of slavery" (Hartman, 2007, p. 6). Angela Davis (1996) wrote, "I choose the word 'abolitionist' deliberately. The 13th Amendment, when it abolished slavery, did so except for convicts. Through the prison system, the vestiges of slavery have persisted" (p. 26). Yet, abolitionist scholar Ruth Wilson Gilmore (in Kushner, 2019) has emphasized that there are important distinctions between slavery and the prison, among them that the prison is primarily a government institution, whereas the plantation was primarily a business with a profit motive. To Gilmore, the difference matters because the prison aims to make use of state funds to separate people from society, rather than investing in social welfare systems like public education, health care, housing, or transport. Geographer Katherine McKittrick (2011) writes that the prison "anticipates . . . the logic that some live, and some die, because this is what nature intended" (p. 956). For abolitionists, ending the prison *entirely* is a prerequisite to building a free and just society.

The United States has been termed a "prison nation" (Herivel & Wright, 2003; Richie, 2012). Although the U.S. prison population has only been formally tracked since 1850, research suggests that the prison population has grown in most years since 1926—nearly a century. As a result of the federal "war on drugs," mandatory minimum sentencing laws, longer sentences, and a variety of other factors, the number of incarcerated people in the United States began to trend sharply upward in 1973 and has since continued, resulting in growth from 241,000 prisoners in 1975 to 1.55 million prisoners in 2010 (Langan, 1991; Pfaff, 2012).[1] The United States imprisons more people than any other country in the world; though it represents just 5% of the world's population, it cages almost 25% of the world's prisoners (Pfaff, 2012). Notably, these statistics do not account for the number of people held in other carceral structures (e.g., local jails, immigration and juvenile detention centers, psychiatric institutions). Though there has been organized resistance against various forms of incarceration since their formation, social movements began to coalesce more strongly around abolishing the prison in the 1960s. These movements were often intertwined with broader struggles for Black liberation, motivated in part by disproportionate rates of Black incarceration (K. Gilmore, 2000). Prison abolition organizing has overlapped with social movements for Indigenous sovereignty (Ogden, 2005), queer/trans justice (Stanley & Smith, 2011; Stanley & Spade, 2012), disability justice (Ben-Moshe, 2013; Piepzna-Samarasinha, 2018), as well as antipoverty and antiracism struggles (e.g., Davis & Rodriguez, 2000; Herivel & Wright, 2003; McLeod, 2019; Richie, 2012; Wang, 2018).

What does all of this have to do with the school? The existence of the prison structures the school, just as it structures other aspects of society. Michel Foucault (1977) argued that structures and practices of schooling served as a means by which to train youth into the disciplinary structures of society. Indeed, the history of carceral residential schooling of Indigenous youth, which separated Indigenous children from their families and attempted to destroy Indigenous languages as part of the ongoing warfare against Indigenous peoples, is an extreme example of this training (Adams, 1995). Education scholar Erica Meiners (2007) and others have suggested that the relationship between schools and prisons is less a linear "pipeline" and more of a "persistent nexus or a web of intertwined, punitive threads" (p. 32). As Meiners describes, this web includes zero-tolerance school discipline policies that mimic criminal law, the punitive surveillance of youth and their communities, and the systems of special education that are associated with negative schooling outcomes like lower graduation rates. In the United States, each of the factors Meiners describes combine to produce what Subini Annamma (2018) terms a "pedagogy of pathologization" that enables the

---

[1] Here, we note that far more social science research has been devoted to measuring the effects of the prison in order to improve it than to exploring its alternatives.

ongoing reproduction of systems of social marginalization. Although the effects of the school–prison nexus may most acutely impact those students whose lives and bodies are viewed as furthest from what a school deems "normal" or "valuable," the pedagogy of pathologization teaches all members of a school community about the kinds of compliance made necessary to avoid punishment, all of which can have profound impacts on a young person's survival, let alone their ability to enjoy learning. As researchers document the disproportionate numbers of Black and Indigenous people of all ages locked behind bars (Burns Institute, 2021; Minton & Cowhig, 2017), we are reminded that understanding carceral systems—in which schooling plays an essential part—means refusing "the reduction of Black and Indigenous to exclusive material, historical, cultural, and ontological categories" (Vaught et al., in press). In other words, the fact that our prison system targets Black and Indigenous peoples challenges us to understand it on conceptual and theoretical terms that reject coloniality and anti-Blackness.

Given the intertwined nature of prisons and schooling, any meaningful engagement with how abolition might inform education raises this question: Does the abolition of the prison require the abolition of the school? Though this question reverberates throughout our study of abolition, we do not have a simple answer. With that said, if theorizing abolition requires us to create the conditions where prisons are no longer necessary, it seems that would necessitate a serious consideration of alternatives to the current structures of public education. As abolitionist scholars Bettina L. Love (2019), Robin D. G. Kelley (2002), and others have written, change requires simultaneous critical analysis and freedom dreaming. We write this chapter in some attempt at both. What is the role of education in creating a society where prisons are obsolete? What is the role of the school in that society, and what is the role of the educational researcher? As former teachers, we are deeply aware of both the restrictions and fugitive possibilities offered by the school (Moten & Harney, 2013). We are largely driven by our commitments to the communities where we worked and the ones we call home, which have historically been deeply harmed by systems of incarceration. As we think about how to proceed with our research and scholarship, we ask, "How might abolition inform educational research?"

Learning in the Present

Though the two of us now live in separate countries, we first met in Oakland, California. Oakland has been a central site of the prison abolition movement, building for at least the last 50 years. Critical Resistance, a national grassroots organizing network of prison abolitionists, was founded there in 1997.

The praxis of abolition has strongly shaped the landscape of community organizing within and around the San Francisco Bay Area, including our own work.

> Harper: have never been inside of a prison. I have never been arrested. Very few people in my life have spent time in jail or prison, most of them not for very long. Prison seems far away from me. At the same time, my entire life is structured by that feeling of distance. Growing up in a predominately White and wealthy family, it never seemed possible that the members of my family who had severe mental health struggles or who committed domestic assault would go to prison. I also know that the prison would only have made those problems worse. In my work as a teacher, I saw the countless ways I was guided to control my students' bodies based on their gender and race—everything started to click. What would we do differently with young people if we were reaching toward a world where prisons were unnecessary?
>
> Kyle: My first trip to Oakland was in 2008 for Critical Resistance's 10-year anniversary convening when I was a college student learning about critical race theory in education. At the convening, I met researchers and activists whose work I had just started reading and learned histories and theories of abolition. Despite having grown up among organizers in Baltimore, this convening was the first time that I heard a land acknowledgement. Later, working in the school system was my entry point in and out of abolitionist study and struggle. Once, I copied a quote from Angela Davis's *Are Prisons Obsolete* (2003) onto a notecard that I taped to my desk as a reminder. It said, "When children attend schools that place a greater value on discipline and security than on intellectual development, they are attending prep schools for prison" (p. 39). While my relationship to abolition has significant roots, I am still very much a student.

In the midst of these times, we have returned to an ongoing conversation about the role of abolition in our work and how we can support education that strengthens youth and their communities. We invite you to join us.

Our Process: Studying Abolition in Relation

Relationships and buildings have a lot in common; they both hold people. And, like buildings, relationships reflect and produce the values and ideas around which they are organized. Our learning about abolition in educational research methodology happens in the context of our relationship and our work within school buildings, which extends onto and beyond the pages of this chapter. As an invitation into our process, we will describe how we organized our collaborative investigation of abolition and educational research methodology in an attempt to push one another as learners. We conducted three semi-structured conversations interspersed with a reflective correspondence about salient themes from those conversations. Our first conversation focused on the theoretical foundations of abolition. We aimed to do a close reading of foundational abolitionist texts, move toward shared understanding of central themes, and discuss how they related to the educational research methodological traditions we work in. In our second conversation, we discussed the methodological implications of abolition based on close reading of scholarship on educational theory and research methodology that explicitly engages abolition. Then, we collaboratively reviewed the transcripts from our first two conversations, individually selected a salient theme, and wrote letters to each other with our thoughts. We reviewed this set of documents to inform a third conversation intended to clearly articulate what we have learned about abolition in educational research through more rigorous engagement with existing scholarship.

Abolition is fundamentally relational. By this, we mean that the relationships among beings—rather than fixed qualities of those beings—shape reality. As Ruth Wilson Gilmore (2007) explains when addressing readers on how to use *Golden Gulag*, without the mutual interaction of agency and structure "there would be no drama, no dynamic, no story to tell" (p. 27). We also understand abolition to be a collective process. So, as coauthors we designed this process in order to highlight our relationship, our individual relationships to the school systems and universities within which we work, and the institutional relationships we had with children and communities in our roles as public school teachers. Through dialogue and written correspondence, we generated a record and an analysis of these relationships.

Our Learning

We identified three overlapping themes on the lessons of abolition for educational research methodology. First, abolition demands scrutiny of prevailing social practice. Second, although methodology might serve abolition, methodology alone will not give us abolition. Third, abolition-compatible methodology highlights existing tensions in social justice research. We hope these themes can shape the methodological commitments of other students of abolition and contribute to a material practice of political imagination within educational research.

Abolition Asks for Scrutiny

Abolitionist writing and organizing challenges oppressive social institutions, like slavery and prison, that are so pervasive—and so powerful—that they can feel permanent. Even more insidiously, these institutions can seem *natural*. Thus, questioning powerful structures that have organized society for generations can easily feel *unnatural*. In the case of prison abolition, even individuals and communities who have been harmed directly by mass incarceration and police violence may find it difficult to imagine public safety that does not rely on prison and policing. Given these circumstances, abolition demands critical analysis of existing social practice that can holistically represent the oppressive forces that shape our current world. Such a nuanced representation is a step toward constructing relationships beyond dominant belief systems that normalize the disposability of human life. Methodology, then, can play a central role in abolition for its potential to "make the familiar strange" (Spindler & Spindler, 2000). At its best, methodology can offer researchers a structure for use in examining everyday practices in ways that excavate their foundational qualities and underlying ideological premises.

In our study of abolition in educational research methodology, we returned to Erica Meiners's scholarship. In Meiners's (2016) critical analysis of the relationship between childhood and carceral networks, she describes coteaching an arts-based participatory action research methods class to high school students. Meiners (2016) explains, "As the attention of the school and the surround[ing] community was focused on violence, not surprisingly the topic this class of sophomore and juniors selected to investigate was safety, particularly school safety" (p. 185). Despite many of their own personal experiences with the harm that police and prisons cause, Meiners reports her students' findings—that more police and more surveillance would increase school safety—to demonstrate the intractability of carceral logics and the difficulty with abolitionist thinking. In our discussion, Kyle reflected:

> In her practice, Meiners *chooses* to teach an open-ended arts-based participatory research methods class. Meiners shows what the students come up with—to focus on this concept of safety—even though she spent the entire book challenging safety as a goal. It makes me wonder about what we ask methods to do, and if the value of methods is distinct from the products that they create. Even if this sort of methodology leads to students coming up with recommendations that are carceral, is it still valuable? Is that an abolitionist method?

Kyle's questions reminded us that abolition is about building for the long term. Abolition-compatible methodology requires that we practice training our gaze upon social structures that are commonly taken for granted. Meiners's methodology invited students into a process of studying structures; even if she did not necessarily agree with their conclusions, the process allowed students to practice critical and collaborative structural inquiry.

Elaborating, Harper shared about adventure playgrounds in an attempt to trace an abolitionist genealogy in education. Adventure playgrounds embrace unrestricted, imaginative play facilitated by tools, paint, and scrap building material rather than adult-made play structures (Kozlovsky, 2008). They proliferated across Europe in the aftermath of World War II as part of a campaign to help young people contribute to building postwar societies. Harper explained:

> Before adventure playgrounds, playgrounds were often heavily monitored by adult facilitators that would teach children how to play. Kids didn't really respond so well to all that. In trying to identify the best materials for children's play, the adults learned—(laughs) what everybody who has ever been around a child knows—that it was mostly the stuff that was just lying around the environment. It was cardboard boxes and trash. It was everything that was already there. That's kind of a nice metaphor for thinking about what's possible for the future. The building blocks are already here, and people are already doing abolitionist work in education all the time. Kids are doing it. Adults are doing it. It's happening. We just need to be looking more carefully and building relationships around it.

Inspired by Harper, Kyle wrote a letter reflecting on its significance for methodology:

> Empiricism, for all its shortcomings, offers a way to rigorously engage with the detritus of the world. At best (and worst) empiricism can structure how we observe the shit our society has produced and, maybe, somewhere in that shit are the building blocks of abolition—if we learn how to play with them.

Here, methodology demands that we look critically and carefully at our present society in order to construct an abolitionist future from the insurgent practices already underway. Educational research methods may be well suited to this task for their focus on teaching and learning between generations. However, this argument has limits. We are not asserting that abolition is a methodological project, but that research methodology can be of service to its broader goals.

Abolition-Compatible Methodology

Methodology is flexible: it sets a course, but not a destination. Abolition, in contrast, is more specific. Prison abolition refers explicitly to the end of the system of incarceration in which individuals are removed from their communities and surveilled and restricted as a form of retribution. Abolishing the police means closing precincts, firing officers, and reallocating budgets toward community-determined investments in health, housing, and jobs. As this tension surfaced in our conversations, Kyle suggested, "I don't think there ever is going to be an abolitionist method, but [methodology] can serve abolitionist goals if it works toward being able to more critically uncover, name, and describe realities that are obfuscated by carceral hegemonies."

Drawing on the work of Critical Resistance, we might call this contingent role for methodology in abolitionist work *abolition-compatible methodology*. Research methodology is abolition-compatible when it aligns with and/or contributes to specific abolitionist struggles. A significant challenge to this alignment comes from the relationship between research and the university. The university has its own history of contributing to carcerality: Its research has expanded surveillance technologies and geographies of destruction. University-based research also belongs, largely, to the increasingly profit-driven institution, and for that reason the abolitionist possibilities are limited. Therefore, it is important for abolition-compatible methodology to take place in relationship with activists working outside of the university. Methodology is not abolitionist, in part, because research can never be a singular driver of abolitionist struggle; it must always be a partner. As Kyle offered later,

> Abolition is a paradigm, right? Like Bettina Love says, it's not an approach—it's a way of approaching work as a researcher. It makes you ask questions like, "What's the purpose of research? What are the skills of a researcher?" or, "What's the role of the researcher in society? What's the purpose of the research once it's completed?" And then, "How does one approach designing a project or answering a question with those ideas in mind?"

Focusing on abolition compatibility in research methodology invites us to join critical scholarship on the supportive role researchers can play in collective work seeking to transform society (Brayboy et al., 2012; Smith, 2012). This is an important reminder that progressive action toward social change must always be collective. Abolition may have an ever-growing syllabus, but it will not have a principal investigator. Abolitionist movements remind us that the kind of social change we seek comes from the sustained, creative work of groups of people rather than from individual leadership.

Abolition Highlights Tension

Abolition-compatible methodology highlights existing tensions in social justice research. In our study, two tensions in particular surfaced: the tension between individual freedom and collective freedom as well as the tension between studying individuals and studying social conditions. To paraphrase what Ruth Wilson Gilmore often says in her public talks, institutions are not actors in and of themselves; institutions are made up of people. *People* build, fund, and staff prisons. *People* send people to jail. Each of those people is or was once a student in a classroom. These are not separate systems.

Ending carceral systems requires us to more carefully envision freedom. As scholars thinking about education as a way of practicing freedom (hooks, 1994/2014), the university settings where we work often illustrate the tensions between education and the institution of schooling. For example, *freedom* is a word we hear a lot on university campuses. These days, we hear it used in association with "free speech" as a rallying cry for White nationalists and transphobic speakers to be granted paid speaking gigs. Sometimes we hear it as a call for "civil discourse" in classrooms, which too often is used as a way of suggesting that oppressed students be polite to those expressing views that support their oppression. We interpret this discourse as an investment in individual freedom without relational accountability; it is a kind of investment in freedom as property, as a stake in stolen ground. In the context of the United States, individual freedom as property may be synonymous with Whiteness as property (Bey, 2020; Harris, 1993).

When we think about freedom, however, we imagine something different. We imagine freedom as what Angela Davis (2016) has termed a "constant struggle." Bringing abolition to education, Bettina Love (2019) writes, "The ultimate goal of abolitionist teaching is freedom. Freedom to create your reality, where uplifting humanity is at the center of all decisions" (p. 89). The tension between different conceptions of an idea like freedom matters for educational research methodology because it contributes to how we understand the people with whom we work as well as how we see our scholarship contributing to broader social goals.

Abolition productively builds tension between studying people and studying social conditions. While much has been said of this split, we are interested in the particular implications of educational research when it presumes to analyze individuals or when it intends to analyze social conditions. As we reread foundational writing by abolitionist scholars, we discussed Angela

Davis's (2003) *Are Prisons Obsolete?* in which Davis describes the meaning of the prison industrial complex:

> The term "prison industrial complex" was introduced by activists and scholars to contest prevailing beliefs that increased levels of crime were the root cause of mounting prison populations. Instead, they argued, prison construction and the attendant drive to fill these new structures with human bodies have been driven by ideologies of racism and the pursuit of profit. (p. 84)

Abolition asks us to look to the root. We observe that, often, methodological focus on individuals uses the idea of individuality to animate dominant narratives rather than nuanced portraits of lived experience. As Harper put it in our conversation,

> Are we studying people and measuring them and trying to understand and draw lines around how they understand themselves? Or are we analyzing the carceral conditions that are structuring their lives in an effort to transform society? At this point, I feel pretty confident in saying that I don't think that most social science research is to be trusted with people's personal experience. It has not earned that.

The tensions that abolition highlights in methodology make us think about the role of *fantasy* in research. Central to discourse of abolition is language around dreaming and reimagining. Indeed, abolition is often critiqued for being "unrealistic." But, as these tensions underscore, hegemony is certainly fantastic in the way that it bends our perception to preexisting tropes. Thinking with abolition in research methodology means interrogating the way scholarship is deployed to validate the fantasies of hegemony.

Conclusion

Taken together, these three themes highlight the importance of addressing *who* or *what* is being strengthened in our research as a methodological problem. We close here with individual reflections on the methodological commitments to abolition we are bringing to our research.

Harper is committed to studying transformative pedagogy, that is, how the ways we teach and learn support or foreclose the possibility of more just futures. As he often says, "Everything is a teacher." People learn from all elements of the world around them, not just from school curricula. We learn from buildings, laws, relationships, land, art, style—the list goes on. Harper is committed to pedagogy because it is a relational form. One of Harper's projects has been to develop the idea of critical trans pedagogy (Keenan, 2017). An abolition-compatible approach to thinking about trans freedom in schools does not prioritize adding legal gender categories or developing antibullying policies that expand systems of punishment. Instead, it seeks new ways to support young people in *being together*. Harper is committed to methodologies that support collaborative inquiry among children, making use of modalities like play and art that enable children to cultivate political imagination toward building new, less harmful social formations.

Kyle is designing a dissertation project that will study language policy and planning in three new public high schools exclusively serving recently arrived immigrants learning English. This ethnographic project asks what language policy in newcomer schools can teach us about the futures we build with and for racialized youth. He will analyze the collision of state-authored language policy with the informal language policy created by immigrant youth that is shaped by their everyday experiences navigating life as new-comers in Southern California. Thinking from an abolitionist framework reminds him that the fact that so much state power is exerted upon regulating language in school demonstrates the insurgent power of youth language (Sojoyner, 2016). So, what does the monitoring of the language of young people teach us about the role of language regulation in the protection of colonial, racial capitalist accumulation? Or, more particularly, how does language policy contribute to the construction of surplus human beings? He will study the actual language practices of young people for what they have to teach us about growing an abolitionist future.

References

Adams, D. W. (1995). *Education for extinction: American Indians and the boarding school experience, 1875–1928*. University Press of Kansas.

Annamma, S. (2018). *The pedagogy of pathologization: Dis/abled girls of color in the school-prison nexus*. Routledge.

Awkward-Rich, C. (2020, January 21). *Meditations in an emergency*. Split This Rock. https://www.splitthisrock.org/poetry-database/poem/meditations-in-an-emergency

Ben-Moshe, L. (2013). Disabling incarceration: Connecting disability to divergent confinements in the USA. *Critical Sociology, 39*(3), 385–403. http://doi.org/10.1177/0896920511430864

Bey, M. (2020). *Anarcho-Blackness: Notes toward a Black anarchism*. AK Press.

Burns Institute. (2021). *United States of disparities: 2017 detention rates for all youth of color*. https://usdata.burnsinstitute.org/#comparison=2&placement=1&races= 2,3,4,5,6&offenses=5,2,8,1,9,11,10&year=2017&view=map

Davis, A. Y. (1996). Incarcerated women: Transformative strategies. *Black Renaissance 1*(1), 21–26. https://www.proquest.com/docview/215530045?pq-origsite=gscholar&fromopenview=true

Davis, A. Y. (2003). *Are prisons obsolete?* Seven Stories Press.

Davis, A. Y. (2016). *Freedom is a constant struggle: Ferguson, Palestine, and the foundations of a movement.* Haymarket.

Davis, A. Y., & Rodriguez, D. (2000). The challenge of prison abolition: A conversation. *Social Justice, 27*(3), 212–218. https://www.jstor.org/stable/29767244?seq=1#metadata_info_tab_contents

Feinberg, L. (1998). *Trans liberation: Beyond pink or blue.* Beacon.

Foucault, M. (1977). *Discipline and punish: The birth of the prison.* Pantheon Books.

Gilmore, K. (2000). Slavery and prison—understanding the connections. *Social Justice, 27*(3), 195–205. https://www.jstor.org/stable/29767242

Gilmore, R. W. (2007). *Golden gulag: Prisons, surplus, crisis, and opposition in globalizing California.* University of California Press.

Harris, C. I. (1993). Whiteness as property. *Harvard Law Review, 106*(8), 1707–1791. https://www.jstor.org/stable/pdf/1341787.pdf

Hartman, S. (2007). *Lose your mother: A journey along the Atlantic slave route.* Farrar, Straus and Giroux.

Hartman, S. (2008). Venus in two acts. *Small Axe, 12*(2), 1–14. https://www.muse.jhu.edu/article/241115

Herivel, T., & Wright, P. (Eds.). (2003). *Prison nation: The warehousing of America's poor.* Psychology Press.

hooks, b. (2014). *Teaching to transgress.* Routledge. (Original work published in 1994)

Keenan, H. B. (2017). Unscripting curriculum: Toward a critical trans pedagogy. *Harvard Educational Review, 87*(4), 538–556. https:doi.org/10.17763/1943-5045-87.4.538

Kelley, R. D. G. (2002). *Freedom dreams: The Black radical imagination.* Beacon.

Kozlovsky, R. (2008). Adventure playgrounds and postwar reconstruction. In M. Gutman & N. de Coninck-Smith (Eds.), *Designing modern childhoods: History, space, and the material culture of children* (pp. 171–190). Rutgers University Press.

Kushner, R. (2019, April 17). Is prison necessary? Ruth Wilson Gilmore might change your mind. *The New York Times Magazine.* https://www.nytimes.com/2019/04/17/magazine/prison-abolition-ruth-wilson-gilmore.html

Langan, P. A. (1991). America's soaring prison population. *Science, 251*(5001), 1568–1573. https://doi.org/10.1126/science.251.5001.1568

Love, B. (2019). *We want to do more than survive: Abolitionist teaching and the pursuit of educational freedom.* Beacon.

McKittrick, K. (2011). On plantations, prisons, and a Black sense of place. *Social and Cultural Geography, 12*(8), 947–963. https://doi.org10.1080/14649365.2011.624280

McLeod, A. M. (2019). Envisioning abolition democracy. *Harvard Law Review, 132*(6), 1613–1649. https://harvardlawreview.org/wp-content/uploads/2019/04/1613-1649_Online.pdf

Meiners, E. R. (2007). *Right to be hostile: Schools, prisons, and the making of public enemies*. Routledge.

Meiners, E. R. (2016). *For the children? Protecting innocence in a carceral state*. University of Minnesota Press.

Minton, T., & Cowhig, M. (2017). *Jails in Indian country, 2016*. U.S. Department of Justice, Office of Justice Programs, Bureau of Justice Statistics. https://www.bjs.gov/content/pub/pdf/jic16.pdf

Moten, F., & Harney, S. (2013). *The undercommons: Fugitive planning and Black study*. Minor Compositions.

Ogden, S. (2005). The prison-industrial complex in Indigenous California. In J. Sudbury (Ed.), *Global lockdown: Race, gender, and the prison-industrial complex* (pp. 57–65). Routledge.

Pfaff, J. F. (2012). Waylaid by metaphor: A deeply problematic account of prison growth. *Michigan Law Review, 111*(6), 1087–1110. https://repository.law.umich.edu/mlr/vol111/iss6/12/

Piepzna-Samarasinha, L. L. (2018). *Care work: Dreaming disability justice*. Arsenal Pulp Press.

Richie, B. (2012). *Arrested justice: Black women, violence, and America's prison nation*. NYU Press.

Smith, L. T. (2012). *Decolonizing methodologies: Research and Indigenous peoples* (2nd ed.). Zed Books.

Sojoyner, D. M. (2016). *First strike: Educational enclosure in Black Los Angeles*. University of Minnesota Press.

Spindler, G., & Spindler, L. (2000). *Fifty years of Anthropology of Education 1950–2000: Spindler anthology*. Erlbaum.

Stanley, E. A., & Smith, N. (2011). *Captive genders: Trans embodiment and the prison industrial complex*. AK Press.

Stanley, E. A., & Spade, D. (2012). Queering prison abolition, now? *American Quarterly, 64*(1), 115–127. https://doi.org/10.1353/aq.2012.0003

Vaught, S., Chin, J. A., Brayboy, B. M. J. (in press). *Conquest carceral education projects: The school-prison trust*. University of Minnesota Press.

Wang, J. (2018). *Carceral capitalism*. MIT Press.

9

METHODOLOGIES FOR GESTURING TOWARDS DECOLONIAL FUTURES

Sharon Stein, Vanessa Andreotti, Cash Ahenakew, Rene Susa, Will Valley, Sarah Amsler, Camila Cardoso, Dino Siwek, Tereza Cajkova, Dani D'Emilia, Ninawa Huni Kui, Mateus Tremembe, Rosa Pitaguary, Benício Pitaguary, Nadia Pitaguary, Ubiraci Pataxó, Lynn Mario Trindade Menezes de Souza, Bill Calhoun, Shawn Van Sluys, Carolina Azul Duque, Kyra Royo Fay, and Ben Lickerman

The Gesturing Towards Decolonial Futures (GTDF) research/arts/ ecology collective is a transnational and intergenerational collaboration among researchers, artists, educators, students, social justice and environmental activists, and Indigenous knowledge keepers. The work of the collective is multifaceted, but one of our primary orienting concerns is to grapple with the difficulties, paradoxes, and complexities that are often involved in efforts to enact systemic change at the intersection of concerns related to ongoing colonial violence and ecological crises. Specifically, we ask how we might pedagogically interrupt and reorient the colonial patterns that tend to be circularly reproduced through mainstream theories of change and approaches to problem-solving (see Andreotti et al., 2021; GTDF Collective, 2020; Stein et al., 2020). The "gesturing" in our name indicates recognition of the fact that decolonization is not a single event but rather an ongoing, nonlinear, long-term process. As GTDF member Elwood Jimmy says, decolonizing work is more like a marathon than a sprint; and in order to prepare for this marathon, we need to develop the endurance, capacities, and stamina that will equip us to face the detours, potholes, and speedbumps that will inevitably arise in this path.

We frame the work of the GTDF collective as a form of *education otherwise* that seeks to become more accountable to the fact that our lives and livelihoods are subsidized by a violent and unsustainable (i.e., colonial) system, while also gesturing toward horizons of hope beyond what is offered by that system (Stein et al., 2020). This system is characterized by

- politics organized by colonial nation-states;
- economics organized by racial capitalism;
- epistemologies organized by "universal" knowledge and reason;
- relationships organized by human exceptionalism, utility, and transactionalism (i.e., relationships premised and evaluated on their perceived costs and benefits); and
- a social ecology organized by a fantasy of separation and hierarchy between humans and the earth ("man" and "nature"), and between humans and each other.

Education otherwise is focused on unlearning these colonial modes of thinking, being, feeling, sensing, desiring, and relating, as well as *learning to be taught by* other ways of thinking, being, feeling, sensing, desiring, and relating without repeating harmful colonial patterns of engagements across difference (including extraction, appropriation, instrumentalization, romanticization, and consumption). In this chapter, we describe how our methodological practices seek to support the process of identifying, interrupting, and "composting" harmful patterns so as to prepare the soil for different configurations of shared existence to grow.

Our research methodology has at least three different dimensions that we distinguish here for pedagogical purposes, although in practice they are highly connected and intertwined. The first dimension is an *intellectual critique* that seeks to bring attention to overlapping forms of systemic social and ecological violence, and to the complexities involved in addressing this violence. Those seeking linear progress, consensus, system continuity, and simple solutions often prefer to ignore these complexities, as well as common tensions, absences, paradoxes, complicities, and difficult questions. The second dimension invites people to "bring the body back" (de Souza, 2019) into decolonizing work and accept responsibility for clearing *affective space.* This affective work is about identifying, denaturalizing, and decluttering the nongenerative defenses, traumas, denials, fears, anxieties, fantasies, and projections that each of us hold within us and that are activated as embodied sensations in response to different external stimuli and social contexts. Decluttering these affective "ditches" can create more space for critiques of systemic violence to land in the body in deeper ways, and for other possibilities to emerge. This part of the work invites people to shift not just their intellectual assumptions but also their conscious and unconscious investments away from harmful promises. The third dimension is a commitment to *relational rigor* in general but especially in the context of research collaborations with communities of high-intensity struggle. This relational rigor is rooted in trust, respect, accountability, consent, and reciprocity (Ahenakew, 2016, 2019; Kirkness & Barnhardt, 1991; Kovach, 2010; Mika, n.d.; Whyte, 2020). Relational rigor orients us toward ensuring the quality and integrity of relationships and focuses on fostering the possibilities that can emerge in the process of weaving different futures together, rather than rushing to achieve predetermined outcomes and assuming that we need to agree on a "single forward." In this chapter, we touch on each of these three dimensions and illustrate how they are integrated within a selection of creative methodologies we have developed through our research practice.

GTDF Collective's Systemic Analysis

The GTDF collective's work is inspired by two primary sources of insight and theoretical direction: first, critiques offered by de-/postcolonial, abolitionist, and critical ethnic studies; second, analyses and practices of communities engaged in high-intensity struggles, in particular those Indigenous communities in Canada, Brazil, Peru, and Mexico that are part of the collective and overlapping networks (the In Earth's CARE network and the Teia de 5 Curas).

In our work, we call "high-intensity" those urgent struggles to defend one's lands, lives, and livelihoods from active threat, while "low-intensity" struggles are generally efforts to ensure more access to resources, representation, and security within the modern/colonial system, or attempts to escape the modern/colonial system by creating alternatives that still depend on the system's violence (see Amsler, 2019). This distinction is not meant to dismiss the importance of low-intensity struggles, as both kinds of struggle are indispensable. However, discussions about the "importance" of one type of struggle over the other tend to invisibilize a qualitative difference between fighting to sustain and expand a system and fighting to survive in the face of the violence that is required to sustain and expand that system.

From these two sources of analysis, we have come to understand our currently dominant global system as a "modern/colonial system" in which modern promises (e.g., political stability, economic security, epistemic certainty, and unrestricted autonomy) are subsidized by colonial processes (e.g., poverty, genocide, exploitation, dispossession, ecological destruction, and cognitive imperialism; Andreotti, 2011; Byrd, 2011; Coulthard, 2014; Mignolo, 2011; Silva, 2014; Spivak, 2004). In this analysis, coloniality is the constitutive but disavowed underside of modernity. In other words, there is no modernity without coloniality, yet this connection is invisibilized in mainstream analyses of social problems and imaginaries of justice, responsibility, and change. For instance, in mainstream analyses poverty is generally framed as the product of a lack of access to universal knowledge and values and a lack of inclusion into modern institutions, infrastructures, and subjectivities. From this perspective, increased access to these knowledges and institutions are framed as straightforward, viable, and desirable "solutions." The modernity/coloniality framework suggests instead that these institutions, infrastructures, and subjectivities are inherently violent and unsustainable—and actually require the impoverishment of some in order to ensure the enrichment of others. Thus, the foundational violence is not the *exclusion* of marginalized communities from the "benefits" of the modern/colonial system, but the fact that those benefits come at the *expense* of those communities and of the wider ecologies that sustain us.

With this analysis, we invite people to sit with the paradox that while expanding access to this system is, in one layer, a move *toward* greater justice, in other layers it is a move *away* from justice, as the true social and ecological costs of the system are always displaced somewhere else (Byrd, 2011). This paradox in turn prompts consideration of the possibility that this system ultimately cannot be reformed, but rather can only be "hospiced" as we face unprecedented overlapping social, ecological, economic, and political crises caused by the system itself.

We use the metaphor of system hospicing to emphasize that our current system may be in a terminal crisis, and if so, we have a responsibility to support it to "die well" (Andreotti et al., 2015; GTDF Collective, 2020; Machado de Oliveira, 2021). At the same time as we hospice the old system, we are also called to the work of supporting the birth of something new that will emerge in its place. We say "supporting the birth," or midwifing, rather than "birthing," not only because this birth is a collective process rather than one defined by a single person or group, but also because we seek to decenter human agency and exceptionalism in this process. Hospicing an old system and midwifing a new one is also not just about what happens outside of us, but also includes sitting with the processes of death and birth inside of ourselves, as we are also part of this system. These two processes of death and birth are different but intertwined in the cycles of life; for instance, if we do not learn from the mistakes of the modern/colonial system, then we will likely reproduce them as we make space for emerging possibilities. In both kinds of work—hospicing and midwifing—there are many opportunities to either make new mistakes (which is inevitable in the process of experimenting with otherwise possibilities) or circularly repeat old mistakes (which suggests continued investment in the promises and securities offered by the previous system). The GTDF collective is focused on developing tools and practices that can support individual and collective capacities and dispositions to identify, interrupt, and be taught by the lessons of these mistakes, and to move collectively toward a way of being grounded on sobriety, maturity, discernment, and accountability (SMDA; the deeper layers of meaning), which we elaborate further next.

Beyond Description-Prescription in Research

Most educational research is oriented by the underlying assumption that it is through acquiring more information that people can change their ideas and values, and based on this shift in values and ideas they will change their actions. We specifically find that much research is made up of two primary elements: a description of a problem, followed by a proposed prescription for what is to be done in order to address that problem (Stein, 2021). This formula creates (and reproduces) certain parameters of what constitutes scholarly legitimacy and intelligibility. This includes the expectations that research will be rooted in a narrative of unidirectional linear progress, in which we are (or should be) perpetually moving toward a "better" (wiser, wealthier, more plural and ethical) future; language is framed as a human tool that can accurately, objectively describe the whole of reality; chosen canonical *or* revolutionary thinkers are exceptional, universal, and above critique; and solutions are to be determined in advance and take on a form that can be replicable and relevant across diverse contexts.

While the specific direction, narrative, language, and thinkers one frames as part of a universal narrative (of descriptions and prescriptions) will vary, in general research is calibrated around these imperatives. Thus, knowledge production is commonly framed as a competition for epistemic (as well as sometimes political and/or moral) authority, and the assumption that whoever has the most accurate, ethical, legitimate, totalizing, objective, and thereby superior mode of describing a problem and prescribing change should be the one to lead it. To produce knowledge that interrupts the notion of a single path forward in which everyone should be invested, or that is not motivated by a desire for epistemic hegemony or universal relevance, is to risk becoming unintelligible or illegitimate to others in the research community and beyond.

Research for Education Otherwise

Description-prescription research is extremely important and has many contextual, provisional uses in facing today's crises. At the same time, we understand that this approach is limited. We also understand that our academic work does not necessarily escape this formula, even as we seek to question it and gesture toward other possibilities. This is another paradox that we cannot simply transcend, but rather must wrestle with in our work. Specifically, we try to do this by inviting people to interrupt their satisfaction not only with the currently available descriptions and prescriptions, but also with their satisfaction with the promise that we could ever find a single description-prescription that will be universally relevant. Instead, we seek to invite engagement with the gifts and limitations of descriptions and prescriptions, thereby acknowledging the contextual relevance of different orientations.

Beyond this, we also invite people to sit at the edge of the currently imaginable ways of knowing and be taught by these limits, but without then simply seeking to replace them immediately or necessarily with other ways of knowing, especially not with a new universal. Education otherwise also invites people to "zoom out" (from their personal contexts and opinions) and see the multiple (often contradictory) layers at work in any given situation, and to consider the different assumptions and implications that accompany all possible analyses and answers. Even as we do this, we also seek to interrupt the common tendency to mistake human-made maps of reality for the territory itself—in other words, acknowledging that reality is always moving and more complex than can be described and discerned, and that there is not only much that is as yet unknown but also much that is simply unknowable.

Generally, it is expected that education must either be teacher centered or learner centered. Within this dialectical framing, there are only two possible options or a compromise synthesis position in between them. As a result, other possibilities are unimaginable and thus fall out of view. Our approach to education otherwise proposes another possibility: centering the earth or the world itself, while understanding that learners and teachers are also *part* of that world and entangled with it. This differs from education that either treats the world as something separate from us that we can codify and impose upon or as something that imposes on us.

Education otherwise seeks to prepare learners with the stamina and the intellectual, affective, and relational capacities to hold space for the complexity, uncertainty, paradoxes, contradictions, and disillusionment that accompany any effort to enact social change or respond to possible social collapse. The idea is to equip learners to identify, interrupt, and deactivate circular colonial patterns and harmful and unsustainable attachments and desires (in oneself and others) with more SMDA. These words (sobriety, maturity, discernment, and accountability) have multiple layers of meaning, but in the context of the work of GTDF, we suggest the following:

- *Sobriety* is about identifying and interrupting (socially conditioned) modern desires and compulsions, including tendencies to demand authority (whether epistemic, moral, or political), arbitration of common sense, and/or affirmation of innocence (three A's).
- *Maturity* is about identifying and interrupting relationship building centered on transactions, projections, and idealizations. It involves decentering the self, disarming defenses, and dis-investing from self-infantilizations in order to witness the reality (including the pain) of a situation (three D's) without turning away or wanting to be rescued from discomfort.
- *Discernment* is about "layering" reality and learning to hold space for complexities, complicities, and contradictions (three C's; within ourselves, within other beings, and within the world) without feeling immobilized, irritated, or overwhelmed.
- *Accountability* is about realizing at whose expense our learning and livelihoods are sustained and mobilizing responsibility toward a commitment to try and reduce and interrupt harm while recognizing that we may fail in our attempts to do so.

Education otherwise also emphasizes the importance of ethically and politically accountable engagements with other theories and practices of education, especially those that have been historically and systemically marginalized within the dominant modern/colonial system. The idea is not that these other possibilities can or should replace the dominant system, but rather that they serve as a reminder that other ways of knowing, being, and relating are viable, albeit unimaginable to many. They also remind us of the colonial violence that has led to these other ways of knowing being delegitimized (Santos, 2007). The challenge is how to facilitate these engagements in ways that don't reproduce harm, especially given that they often take place at the interface between communities of low- and high-intensity struggle that are unevenly positioned, which can lead to the colonial patterns of tokenism, appropriation, instrumentalization, consumption, extraction, erasure, and romanticization of difference.

Much of our work is done in the context of low-intensity struggles, that is, among those who have been relatively structurally advantaged within the modern/colonial system, and especially among those seeking to extend and expand that system. In these contexts, we have found that a primary challenge to interrupting investment in system continuity is not a lack of information about the true costs of the modern promises (i.e., the colonial processes that subsidize them). Indeed, many people can theoretically grasp the relationship between modern promises and colonial processes. However, this analytical understanding does not necessarily translate into an interruption or a reorientation of people's desire for the perpetuation and even expansion of those promises. In fact, these desires tend to foreclose the possibility of deep, self-reflexive, and generative engagements with the limits of the existing system.

Generally, we have found that the traditional academic research strategies—of describing the problem and then prescribing a predetermined solution from within available frames of reference—have been inadequate for interrupting and reorienting harmful desires. This is because these desires are often sustained through unconscious affective investments, patterns, and constellations that are not responsive to rational, political, or moral argument. When we try to address these problems directly or descriptively, we often meet significant resistance and strategies of further denial, deflection, delegitimization, and defensiveness. Thus, we have oriented our research toward developing pedagogical strategies and practices that can bypass or disarm common defenses and that can prompt people to develop a suspicion about the presumed innocence and benevolence of their own assumptions and desires. This approach follows Spivak's (2004) decolonial psychoanalytic orientation to education as an "uncoercive rearrangement of desires" (p. 256), that is, an interruption of people's existing satisfactions with the modern/colonial system, and an invitation to disinvest from that system, rather than an effort to compel people to disinvest (i.e., through moral posturing, political policing, or the invocation of guilt or shame), or determine for them how they might do that work or foster other possibilities.

Informed by this decolonial psychoanalytic pedagogical approach, our methodological practice often results in the creation of critical and creative social cartographies, metaphors, and other pedagogical, artistic, and collaborative tools and practices that gesture toward education otherwise. Each of these efforts seeks to unsettle sedimented logics, and to map the limits of what is socially sanctioned as imaginable, real, natural, desirable, and possible. We seek to produce knowledge and practices that invite people to disinvest from a sense of unrestricted autonomy, exceptionalism, exaltedness, and entitlement and activate a sense of sobriety, maturity, discernment, and accountability toward an entangled world, which we are all part of (which is rooted in desires to facilitate movement away from further harm and toward healing and collective well-being). Further, we invite people to engage this work with honesty, humility, humor, and hyper-self-reflexivity. In this way, following Santos (2007), we approach knowledge production not as a representation of reality but rather an intervention into reality, which can mobilize viable but unimaginable possibilities for decolonial futures.

Critical and Creative Metaphors, Social Cartographies, and Practices

Our approach to research is often unintelligible to those who are operating from within the mainstream description-prescription formula. In other cases, we find that people are only engaging with our invitation to disrupt satisfactions with harmful desires and move toward responsibility at an intellectual layer, thereby cognitively engaging with the affective and relational layers, but not actually shifting in these layers. When people approach our work without a commitment to affective decluttering and relational rigor, we find that they tend to consume the intellectual critique we offer selectively based on what is convenient (i.e., what they want to do based on what looks and feels good) rather than based on responsibility (i.e., what needs to be done and what they can do). In order to invite movement in the affective and relational layers, more than simply an intellectual description of the problem is needed. This is why the collective is so focused on inviting people to engage with but also beyond their intellect. In this section, we review two of the pedagogical tools that we have created and invite readers to engage them in order to see what these tools can move within them, and how. These are not intended as accurate, fixed representations of reality, but rather as stimuli to loosen existing assumptions and attachments and invite people to see the many layers, implications, and accountabilities that are at work in any particular context or problem of concern (including intellectual, affective, relational, economic, political, and ecological layers, as well as the multiple different dimensions that exist within each of these layers). Each of these tools is a living experiment, meaning that they are never fixed or firm and are instead constantly revised by us and others depending on what is demanded by specific contexts and what else is emerging.

The Bus Metaphor and Methodology

We have found that in order to engage in the work of affective decluttering and relational rigor in generative and generous ways, it is necessary to learn to sit with our own internal complexities, contradictions, and incoherences. In this way, we can become more comfortable with the complexities, contradictions, and incoherences of others, of the world itself, and of efforts to make social change—especially decolonial change. Together this might make us better prepared to hold space for difficult conversations and processes that include elements of conflict, dissensus, failure, and incommensurability. However, this approach is counterintuitive, as it contrasts with mainstream imperatives to emphasize consensus, sameness, and harmony. Similarly, the capacity for accepting complexities, contradictions, and incoherences is generally underdeveloped among those socialized in Western institutions, as these institutions tend to prioritize coherence, certainty, and objectivity. In response to this general lack of capacity and endurance for the "marathon" work of decolonization, we created the "bus" methodology.

The bus methodology (as shown in Figure 9.1) is rooted in a metaphor premised on the notion that each of us has many different "passengers" within us. The bus challenges the notion that we are or should be coherent in how we think, feel, and act. While usually there is only one "driver" at a time, other passengers make themselves known through their thoughts, ideas, and embodied responses to different stimuli. Usually, we are somewhat familiar with the passengers and potential drivers who are closer to the front of the bus and less familiar with those closer to the back.

To use the bus methodology, we invite people to first learn to sit with and observe the different passengers on their bus. We tend to suppress those passengers who embody our shadow sides. For instance, for people who see themselves as committed to decolonization work, the suppressed passengers will be those deeply attached to desires or entitlements that we know are harmful and colonial. However, the invitation of the bus methodology is to become familiar with and accept (without endorsing) *all* of the passengers within ourselves: the good, the bad, the ugly, the broken, and the messed up. The more we know about our passengers, the better able we are to consider

Figure 9.1. The bus methodology.

how they affect ourselves and others, and perhaps recalibrate them and how they express themselves (rather than try to repress them). Ultimately, this can support us to move toward maturity: decentering our egos, deactivating our presumed entitlements and exceptionalism, disarming our defenses, and decluttering our harmful desires and projections.

When people start to feel overwhelmed by a conversation or a stimulus, we invite them to pause and observe which passengers are emerging and how they are responding to things, noticing their presence and their responses without judgment, endorsement, or attachment. One question to ask is, "Which passengers are making themselves known right now?" and then ask subsequent questions: "What are they saying, thinking and feeling? Do each passenger's feelings align with their thoughts, or are they somewhat contradictory? Are they responding from a place of fragility, trauma, or insecurity? What are they projecting onto others? How old are they? How comfortable are they with uncertainty? What is surprising about which passengers emerged and what they felt or said? How do the passengers interact with each other? What does each passenger need (and how does this differ from what they might want)?" People can also ask themselves more general questions about the state of their bus: "Is the bus okay, is it processing, or is there something 'burning' inside of it that needs to be expressed and witnessed, or even 'vomited' out (when roads get rough or windy)? If so, how and with whom is it appropriate to vent or vomit (who can hold a vomit bucket for you without being harmed in the process)? What processing can be done on one's own? What is the terrain like around the bus, and how is that affecting the passengers? What external resources and metabolic processes are required in order to keep the bus 'running,' and how can we both ensure these needs are met and become more accountable for the impacts of those resources and processes on other beings?"

There are many other layers and possibilities for working with the bus metaphor and methodology. This includes, for instance, acknowledging the different decks of the bus. However, for the purposes of this chapter we emphasize that the first step in this methodology is about becoming more familiar with at least one deck of our own buses and holding space for all the passengers on this deck. This can start to create a container for the tensions, dissensus, plurality, and conflict that tend to arise in decolonizing work that enables us to address these in more generative ways. In the following section we offer a stimulus with which readers can practice observing their buses.

"Why I Can't Hold Space for You Anymore" Poem

Those involved in high-intensity struggles have drawn attention to how the bulk of the affective, relational, and pedagogical labor of decolonization is often placed on their shoulders, and how this labor often goes unrecognized and uncompensated. Thus, when working with those engaged in low-intensity struggles, we consider how to activate a sense of responsibility that is not rooted in guilt, shame, paternalism, or desires for absolution, affirmation, or innocence. We have found a significant gap between people's intellectual ability to acknowledge colonial violence in the abstract and their affective and relational abilities to identify and interrupt when they or others embody these patterns in practice. In other words, while we may see ourselves as open and understanding, when faced with a response or position that provokes dissonance, our response usually indicates areas for further *affective* and *relational* depth, and areas where we are still learning to become more SMDA.

The following critical and creative poem was written by the GTDF collective to draw attention to the uneven distribution of labor in the context of decolonization and "imagining otherwise" efforts, and the emotional and embodied costs of this labor for those who are disproportionately asked to perform it. It was written as a synthesis of what frustrated Indigenous and racialized members of the collective have lived through and what they would like to say to their White colleagues and peers, and even occasionally to White members of the collective itself.

When we present this poem, we generally invite people to read it while paying attention to the different kinds of responses that it evokes in them, or on their "bus." Especially for White people, who are implicated by the poem's critique, we ask them to attend to the fears, insecurities, and desires that could be behind these responses, and how these fears, insecurities, and desires could be unconsciously driving these responses and thereby impacting the quality of their relationships with racialized and Indigenous people and communities.

Do You Really Want to Know Why I Can't Hold Space for You Anymore?
Because
You see my body as an extension of your entitlements

Because
I have held space for you before
and every time, the same thing happens
You take up all the space
and expect me to use my time, energy and emotion
in service of fulfilling your desires:
to perform my trauma
to affirm your innocence

to celebrate your self-image
to center your feelings
to absolve you from guilt
to be always generous and generative
to filter what I say in order not to make you feel uncomfortable
to validate you as someone who is good and innocent
to be the appreciative audience for your self-expression
to provide the content of a transformative learning experience
to make you feel loved, important, special and safe
and you don't even realize you are doing it
and you don't even realize you are doing it
AND YOU DON'T EVEN REALIZE YOU ARE DOING IT

Because your support is always conditional
On whether it aligns with your agenda
On whether it is requested in a gentle way
On whether I perform a politics that is convenient for you
On whether it fits your personal brand
On whether it contributes to your legacy
On whether you will get rewarded for doing it
On whether it feels good
Or makes you look good
Or gives you the sense that we are "moving forward"

Because when you "give" me space to speak
It comes with strings attached about
what I can and cannot say
and about how I can say it
You want an easy way out
A quick checklist or one-day workshop
on how to avoid being criticized
while you carry out business as usual

And even when I say what I want to say anyway
You can't hear it
Or you listen selectively
And when you think you hear it
You consume it
You look for a way to say "that's not me"
"I'm one of the good ones"
and use what I say to criticize someone else

Or you nod empathetically and emphatically to my face and then
The next thing you do shows that while you can repeat my words
Your perceived entitlements remain exactly the same

And when I put my foot down or show how deeply angry or frustrated I am
You read me as ungrateful, incompetent, unreliable and betraying your
confidence
You complain behind my back that I'm creating a hostile environment
You say I'm being unprofessional, emotional, oversensitive
That I need to get over it
That I'm blocking progress
That I shouldn't be so angry
That my ancestors lost the battle
That not *everything* is about colonialism or racism or Whiteness
That aren't we all just people, in the end?
That we are all Indigenous to some place
That you feel really connected to the earth, too
That you have an Indigenous friend/colleague/girlfriend that really likes you. . .
You minimize and further invisibilize my pain

Your learning
your self-actualization
your credibility
your security
and your social mobility
always come at my expense.
That is why I can't hold space for your anymore.

In addition to asking people to observe the passengers on their bus while
reading the poem, we also invite them to pause and consider the following: What are the costs of the patterns in the poem in the long run both for
the well-being of those engaged in high-intensity struggle and for the depth
and sustainability of the relationships you build? What would you need to
unlearn to enable healthier and more generative relationships? How does
the expectation that Indigenous and racialized people will offer their time
and intellectual, affective, and relational labor prioritize the learning and
well-being of those in dominant positions? How does this expectation also
invisibilize and ignore the fact it often requires marginalized people to relive
painful and traumatic experiences and frustrations? How could the labor that
is expected of Indigenous and racialized people be better acknowledged or
better yet, (re)distributed in your own context?

Having encountered this poem, some people feel overwhelmed, or immobilized, and seek quick solutions or checklists for how to engage differently, none of which are suitable for the "marathon" work of decolonization. Instead, we invite people to consider what they are learning from observing their bus passengers' response to the poem; to practice sitting with the difficulties and discomforts of this work; and to continually ask the question "What is the next, most responsible, small thing that I can do to work toward weaving more generative relationships rooted in trust, respect, reciprocity, accountability, and consent?"

Conclusion

In this chapter, we have sought to share some of the decolonial directions that underpin the research methodology of the GTDF collective and have offered examples of how this research leads to the development of creative and critical pedagogical metaphors, cartographies, and frameworks. It is important to mention that space and medium restrictions prevent us from introducing the artistic, embodied, and land-based practices that also result from our research. We have outlined the ways that our approach to knowledge production is oriented not by an attempt to describe reality, nor prescribe specific solutions or alternatives, but rather by experimental efforts to map, interrupt, and reorient enduring harmful and unsustainable colonial patterns. This often entails encouraging individual and collective unraveling of the affective knots (e.g., fragilities, fears, projections) that prevent alternative possibilities for knowing, being, and relating from taking root and growing. We have also emphasized that our approach to knowledge production is committed to both intellectual and relational rigor, which means both attending to the geo- and biopolitics of knowledge (i.e., whose knowledge is understood to be normal, legitimate, legible), as well as cultivating collaborations premised on trust, accountability, reciprocity, respect, and consent with those who feel called to do this type of work.

Because the kind of work that we do is ongoing, open-ended, and iterative, it is very difficult to offer the kind of conclusions that people generally hope for. Our pedagogical tools, frameworks, and cartographies seek to foster generative movement at the intellectual, affective, and relational layers of knowledge production and knowledge mobilization, and beyond. This can be difficult as we navigate our different responsibilities in these layers, as well as the political, ecological, and economic layers. Sometimes this leads to internal tensions within the collective itself, for instance in relation to priorities or directions of our collaborative work, but we nonetheless seek to create spaces in which we can have difficult conversations without our relationships falling apart, and in which we can support the work of imagining and enacting more sober, mature, discerning, and accountable possibilities for collective existence.

To conclude, therefore, we offer one final pedagogical tool, which is a set of "hyper-self-reflexivity questions" that we developed to support "peer review" of the work produced by members of the collective, but which we have found to be a useful tool to support the continued learning of those engaged in low-intensity struggles in many different contexts. We especially emphasize the need to learn from our mistakes and failures so that we do not repeat them.

Consider these hyper-self-reflexivity questions:

- In what ways might you be reproducing what you critique?
- To what extent are you avoiding looking at your own complicities, denials, and colonial desires, and at whose expense?
- What are you doing this for? Who are you accountable to? What is your theory of change? What would you like your work to move in the world?
- Who is your imagined audience? What do you expect from this audience? What compromises have you had to make in order for your work to be intelligible and relatable to this audience? To what extent can these compromises compromise the work itself? How can you become more accountable for these compromises? Who are you choosing not to upset and why? How does integrity manifest in your work?
- To what extent are you aware of how you are being read by communities of high-intensity struggle? Who (in these communities) would legitimately roll their eyes at what you are doing (e.g., find it indulgent, self-infantilizing, paternalistic, ethnocentric)?
- Who/what is this really about? Who is benefitting the most from this work?
- To what extent is your work based on the modern grammar of exceptionalism, entitlements, and exaltedness that characterize political engagements within modernity?
- How wide is the gap between where you think you are at and where you actually are? Who would be able to help you realize the extent of that gap? Would you be able to listen?
- To what extent can you respond with humility, honesty, humor, and hyper-self-reflexivity when your work or self-image are challenged?
- What is the next, most responsible, small thing you can do to go deeper in this work?

References

Ahenakew, C. (2016). Grafting Indigenous ways of knowing onto non-Indigenous ways of being. *International Review of Qualitative Research, 9*(3), 323–340. s://doi.org/10.1525/irqr.2016.9.3.323

Ahenakew, C. (2019). *Towards scarring our collective soul wound.* Musagetes Foundation.

Amsler, S. (2019). Gesturing towards radical futurity in education for alternative futures. *Sustainability Science, 14*(4), 925–930. https://doi.org/10.1007/s11625-019-00679-8

Andreotti, V. (2011). *Actionable postcolonial theory in education.* Springer.

Andreotti, V., Stein, S., Suša, R., Cajkova, T., Pitaguary, R., & Pitaguary, B. (2021). *Calibrating our vital compass: Unlearning colonial habits of being in everyday life.* Rizoma Freireano. http://www.rizoma-freireano.org/calibrating-our-vital

Andreotti, V. D. O., Stein, S., Ahenakew, C., & Hunt, D. (2015). Mapping interpretations of decolonization in the context of higher education. *Decolonization: Indigeneity, Education & Society, 4*(1). https://jps.library.utoronto.ca/index.php/des/article/view/22168

Byrd, J. A. (2011). *The transit of empire: Indigenous critiques of colonialism.* University of Minnesota Press.

Coulthard, G. S. (2014). *Red skin, white masks: Rejecting the colonial politics of recognition.* University of Minnesota Press.

de Souza, L. M. T. M. (2019). Decolonial pedagogies, multilingualism and literacies. *Multilingual Margins, 6*(1), 9–13. https://doi.org/10.14426/mm.v6i1.135

Gesturing Towards Decolonial Futures Collective. (2020). *Preparing for the end of the world as we know it.* Open Democracy. www.opendemocracy.net/en/oureconomy/preparing-end-world-we-know-it/

Kirkness, V. J., & Barnhardt, R. (1991). First Nations and higher education: The four R's—Respect, relevance, reciprocity, responsibility. *Journal of American Indian Education*, 30(3), 1–15. https://www.jstor.org/stable/24397980

Kovach, M. (2010). *Indigenous methodologies: Characteristics, conversations, and contexts.* University of Toronto Press.

Machado de Oliveira, V. (2021). *Hospicing modernity: Facing humanity's wrongs and the implications for social activism.* North Atlantic Books.

Mignolo, W. (2011). *The darker side of western modernity: Global futures, decolonial options.* Duke University Press

Mika, C. (n.d.). Indigenous notions of interconnection and formation by the world. In G. W. Noblit (Ed.), *Oxford research encyclopedia of education.* Oxford University Press. https://doi.org/10.1093/acrefore/9780190264093.013.1558

Santos, B. D. S. (2007). Beyond abyssal thinking: From global lines to ecologies of knowledges. *Review (Fernand Braudel Center), 30*(1), 45–89. https://www.jstor.org/stable/40241677

Silva, D. F. D. (2014). Toward a Black feminist poethics: The quest(ion) of Blackness toward the end of the world. *The Black Scholar, 44*(2), 81–97. https://doi.org/10.1080/00064246.2014.11413690

Spivak, G. C. (2004). Righting wrongs. *The South Atlantic Quarterly, 103*(2–3), 523–581. https://doi.org/10.1215/00382876-103-2-3-523

Stein, S. (2021). Reimagining global citizenship education for volatile, uncertain, complex and ambiguous (VUCA) times. *Globalisation, Socieites and Education, 19*(4), 482–495. https://doi-org.ezproxy1.lib.asu.edu/10.1080/14767724.2021 .1904212

Stein, S., Andreotti, S., Hunt, D., Suša, R., Amsler, S., Ahenakew, C., Jimmy, E., Cardoso, C., Siwek, D., Čajková, T., Pitaguary, B., Pataxo, U., Valley, W., D'Emilia, D., & Okano, H. (2020). Gesturing towards decolonial futures: Reflections on our learnings thus far. *Nordic Journal of Comparative and International Education, 4*(1), 43–65. http://doi.org/10.7577/njcie.3518

Whyte, K. (2020). Too late for Indigenous climate justice: Ecological and relational tipping points. *Wiley Interdisciplinary Reviews: Climate Change, 11*(1), e603, 1–7. https://doi.org/10.1002/wcc.603

AFTERWORD

Before, After, During the 100-Year Weave

K. Wayne Yang

Amanda and Z gathered gorgeous voices into this book, and they organized them into Before, During, and After. These simple and profound headings were a *koan* to me, provoking questions rather than promulgating answers and taxonomies. I wondered, *Before, During and After what? For whom? Where?* I loved how I could read these headings many different ways: speculatively, before, during, after decolonization; personally, the before, during, after of my own education; and resistantly, who is to say what counts as before, during, or after!? In this book, I felt the chapters weave together in ways that suggested many directions in the fabric of time, from the before to the after, and back again, during and enduring.

Leigh Patel and I collaboratively drew the foreword and afterword of this book by tracing the warp and weft of these writings. We agreed to let our thoughts travel across the broad distance of the cloth, and not to cover every square inch of it. My thoughts are partial, and I was unable to shout out every chapter in the book, this time. I often tell my students, "Your writing is more than black ink on paper—it is in your heart, in your mind, in the conversations between us." I am holding the teachings from all of the authors in this book in my heart and in my mind, even if they are not in print before you. I imagine you too, reading from your own places, with the times on your mind, and holding your peoples in your heart. I invite you to follow the threads in this book where they lead you, and to weave them into your own story.

I traced a thread in Sam Museus and Amy Wang's "Refusing Neoliberal Logics in Research Design." In transparency, I am here with them, in the alienation of the same institution, built on Kumeyaay land in what people call San Diego. Also, I am asian, an American condition that I share with a few of the writers in this volume, although our histories and experiences and identities are so very different. As settler and not Black, and paid/privileged/ overworked by the university, I was filled with wonder by the ways decolonization, abolition, Indigenous sovereignty, and pro-Blackness filled all the pages of this book, across the varied gendered-raced-classed-placed differences of the writers—yet differently. This sense of wonder made me ask, How do our differences help us unlearn our colonial training and relearn our decolonizing powers? Sam and Amy write across their differences, as advisor and advisee, among others, about what is not talked about in graduate school training. Academia's hidden curriculum is our inculcation into the neoliberal paradigm of individualistic, competitive productivity—a toxin that slowly seduces some or rapidly poisons others. Let us share antidotes to this poison that we have gathered, recipes invented out of survival.

Graduate school is a kind of before—before the hunger games' goal of securing a tenure-track job. Yet I think about before this before. Before we were recruited into the academy, many of us viewed the university with great suspicion and modest hope. Before, we had organic teachers who pushed us toward school, while understanding that they may be pushing us away from our communities. At some point, we become those teachers ourselves. As teachers, we weave a passed-down survivance pattern: voicing the warnings to our students yet singing of an otherwise. We pray that their future in and out of school is not a mirror of the harms that we experienced. Sam and Amy quote bell hooks, who in her writing describes how school was liberation for her as a child, even as it was alienating as a graduate student. I remember Scott Lyons's witty stories about his uncle who ran away from boarding school and his aunt who made everyone go to college. With intention and some meditation, we can move away from individualistic training toward remembering what was before and beyond institutionalized learning. We can join collectivities within and without the academic partitions. We are here in this paradox for a purpose.

As scholars, we are not supposed to gush, but here I go. I loved, "If you can't go to Bella Noche's." Reginald Blockett, Leonard Taylor, Jr., and Steve Mobley, Jr. made me think, yet again, about how Black place-making is belonging-making in a landscape of displacement, and vice versa. Black belonging-making is place-making. I hope this does not sound obvious, because it really is not for me. I think about the premise of the name of The Black/Land Project, founded and sustained by Mistinguette Smith. The forward slash (/) is both bridge and schism of Black-Land relationships. Black people have deep, Indigenous relationships to land. Settler colonialism is anti-Black, characterized by attempts to sever this relationship, over and again. How then is the Black body, in the flesh and in the clearing and in the wake and on the shoals, a place-maker rather than a place-taker?

By flesh, I am drawing from Hortense Spillers's always provoking piece about Blackness and flesh. Spillers teaches us that the corporeal component of anti-Blackness cannot be reduced to "phenotype": It is not just discrimination based on visual appearance; anti-Blackness is actuarial, geo-graphical, nomenclatorial. Anti-Blackness is the business. It is the actuarial mathematics of counting Black bodies as property, as populations to be man-aged, as matter to be disposed of and not counting them as people who matter. It is the creation of entire geographies zoned for Black exclusion, or containment, or death. It is the legal, literary, and scientific nomenclature that calls Black people out of their name and into taxonomies of abjection. Yet Spillers also suggests that Blackness is ontological resistance and insist-ence on being. Black being is a recounting not an accounting, place-making not place-taking, naming relations not taxonomical claiming. By the clear-ing, I am referring to Tiffany King referring to Toni Morrison. In *Beloved,* Morrison narrates "the Clearing—a wide-open place cut deep in the woods nobody knew for what" where Baby Suggs, holy, would hold ceremony for Black life, Black flesh, and Black love. King takes Morrison's metaphor of the "Clearing" to outline a Black liberatory politics of creating fugitive spaces of gathering on Indigenous land. She compellingly teaches us how the clearing is a different symbol for Black life than it is for white settlement—a symbol of communion not conquest. *In the Wake* is one of Christina Sharpe's many gifts to Black thought. *The wake* refers to holding space for the living who are holding space for the dead; the wake also describes, in the invisible, shock waves of anti-Black violence; and it refers to "wake work," the holding of loved ones against the murderous hold of the cell. The Shoals are another formulation by Tiffany King, a name for where Native and Black positionali-ties meet—in the nether land of collected debris near the shore—the shoals that impede the colonizer's pace toward conquest and settlement. I feel the weavings of these Black matters of flesh, clearing, wake, and shoals in the Black queer world-making of Bella Noche's.

Bella Noche's happens "during" the space of academic abjection yet also transcends it—a made-place by Black, queer collectivity, a who of flesh capa-ble of conjuring themselves wherever and whenever, a during and enduring place. Black, queer, and trans practices of gathering and being Black together transform stolen land into liberated place, return stolen bodies into peopled congregations. Bella Noche's, as both place and displacement, a "now here" nowhere, a fugitive refuge, an account, a geo-graph, a named relation. . . . I'm feeling this chapter, and I hope you do as well.

Angie Morrill and Leilani Sabzalian make me think about the practical question facing Native scholars: How do we show up sovereign? How to refuse as needed, to engage as needed, a colonial institution on Indigenous lands that still holds your kin captive, that at best recognizes you as a diver-sity problem? *And return my ancestors. I'll cover shipping.* Angie, Leilani, and the Native women they describe refuse to put sovereignty on hold, despite the university's inability to recognize them as sovereign. For we who are not Native, where can we interrupt our institutional modes of supremacist knowing, so to compel universities into nation-to-nation relations with Indigenous peoples? After colonization and after all, it is Indigenous land beneath and beyond the university where survivance, recognition, and kin-making still happen.

I did not expect to run into Angie and Leilani in this volume. My joy in reading their chapter was akin to being invited to a party by really cool hosts, maybe feeling a little intimidated or worried that one is not quite dressed for the occasion, only to find that your friends are their friends too, a party that becomes a family reunion. Although not Native, I have survivance stories and practices of recognition shared with both these Native feminist writer-teacher-mothers. One that comes to mind is the buddy road trip. Angie and I taught a good number of classes together, and they always transcended boundaries of academic space and time—the way a midsemester, intergalactic buddy road trip might feel. You may practice this survivance strategy yourself. Perhaps you break away from school at times—for an impromptu road trip to Vegas or to the mountains, or for a family ceremony, or to visit a friend who is hurting 500 miles away. Your goal is to collapse that distance, to break out of the university, to rematriate your body, mind, time. Your rusty car or rental vehicle becomes the portal both across that time and to those places, and also out of time. One of our companions, F*king Sam Jung, named this between place where we are together with time-traveling ancestors "the Specularity."

In the buddy trip with Angie that I remember, PattyPark was with us, and she almost fought three douchebags. We had stopped at a waystation for Cheetos or cigarettes or gas. They started mouthing misogynist platitudes about Angie. I tried to stop PattyPark, me characteristically fearful of landing in jail or fists landing on my face. But she kept telling them off until they slunk away. Angie, who is often tuned to fight-or-flight duty for others, was smiling and not caring, her cruise control set to imperturbable. *If I cared what people said about me, I would never leave the house.* There is no academic language to describe this feeling, of anger beyond allyship, of comfort in company, of rag-tag difference that makes kinship. Let us keep us that way, illegible and unintelligible.

My little brother calls my rusty car of 25 years the millennium falcon. When I fly alone today in the afterward of our epic trips, I always think of Angie, and Patty, and you who ride or die. We who were time-traveling dogs together, I recognize you recognize me.

I write in a time of global grief. I thank Leigh, who loved me enough that I could thatch a few words for our collective bookends to this powerful collection of writings. I thank Amanda and Z, who were paragons of patience and compassion. I couldn't write this afterword. But then Leigh told me that Bob Moses reminded her, reminds us, that this is a hundred years' organizing effort. "This" has many names: Perhaps this is justice, perhaps this is decolonization, perhaps this is liberation, perhaps this is the otherwise. We write these bookends to *Weaving an Otherwise*, that they might be less ends and more portals to this, our collective weaving. The practice of weaving applies to cloth, but also to ceremonial braids, to plant medicines, to houses, to boats, to baskets. These are weaves that hold us, sing ceremony with us, heal our spirits and bodies, shelter us, transport us, and help us carry life to others. In the basket weave, the before, during, and after wind toward each other. The hundred-year weave continues, not onward nor afterward, but toward.

References

I deliberately did not insert citations into the body of this essay. These writings informed the whole piece, more than a piecemeal idea here or there.

Black/Land Project. (n.d.). *Home page.* http://www.blacklandproject.org/

Franconia Sculpture Park. (2021, March 29). *Super futures haunt qollective.* https://www.franconia.org/super-futures-haunt-qollective/

hooks, b. (1994). *Teaching to transgress.* Routledge.

Kimmerer, R. W. (2013). *Braiding sweetgrass: Indigenous wisdom, scientific knowledge, and the teachings of plants.* Milkweed Editions.

King, T. J. (2013). *In the clearing: Black female bodies, space and settler colonial landscapes* (Order No. 3599615) [Doctoral dissertation, University of Maryland, College Park]. ProQuest Dissertations & Theses Global.

King, T. L. (2019). *The Black shoals: Offshore formations of Black and Native studies.* Duke University Press.

Lyons, S. R. (2010). *X-marks: Native signatures of assent.* University of Minnesota Press.

Morrill, A. (2017). Time traveling dogs (and other Native feminist ways to defy dislocations). *Cultural Studies ↔ Critical Methodologies, 17*(1), 14–20. https://doi.org/10.1177/1532708616640564

Morrison, T. (1987). *Beloved.* Knopf.

Philip, M. N., & Boateng, S. A. (2008). *Zong!* Wesleyan University Press.

Sharpe, C. E. (2016). *In the wake: On Blackness and being.* Duke University Press.

Spillers, H. J. (1987). Mama's baby, papa's maybe: An American grammar book. *Diacritics, 17*(2), 65–81. https://doi.org/10.2307/464747

ABOUT THE AUTHORS

Reginald Blockett is an assistant professor of higher education at Grand Valley State University. His research centers on the sociocultural experiences of lesbian, gay, bisexual, trans,* and queer collegians of color; Black sexual cultures in postsecondary contexts; and queer of color world-making in college and beyond.

Zachary Brown is a PhD candidate in the Center for the Study of Higher Education at the University of Arizona. His research works within Black critical theory, gender and sexuality studies, and psychoanalytic thought to examine issues of power and desire within and beyond educational contexts.

Grace A. Chen holds a PhD in learning, teaching, and diversity from Vanderbilt University. A former secondary school mathematics teacher, she studies how, why, and what mathematics teachers learn about race, power, and equity, with particular interests in identity, ethics, and affect.

T. Elon Dancy II is Helen S. Faison endowed chair and executive director of the Center for Urban Education at the University of Pittsburgh. His seven books and nearly 100 journal articles, book chapters, and essays broadly explore education settings as sites of African diasporic struggle and world-making, with a focus on Black American populations. More specifically, Dancy studies masculinity formations, power and identity construction, and anti-Blackness in education and society. His research and scholarship have been funded by several foundations and agencies, including the Spencer Foundation, the National Science Foundation, and the McElhattan Foundation. Dancy currently serves as associate editor of *Educational Researcher*.

Kirsten T. Edwards is faculty in the department of Educational Policy Studies, as well as affiliate faculty for African and African diaspora studies and women's and gender studies at Florida International University in Miami, Florida. She currently serves as a diversity mentor professor in the Office of the Vice Provost to Advance Women, Equity & Diversity.

The Gesturing Towards Decolonial Futures Collective is a transnational collective of researchers, artists, educators, students, and activists dedicated to addressing the interrelated challenges of racism, colonialism, unsustainability, climate change, economic instability, mental health crises, and intensifications of social and ecological violence. The collective produces pedagogical, artistic, and cartographic experiments that seek to support healthier possibilities for (co)existence that are viable but are unfathomable from within dominant frames of reference.

Kyle Halle-Erby is a PhD candidate in social research methodology at the University of California, Los Angeles. He studies language policy and planning in compulsory schools for recently arrived immigrant students.

Harper B. Keenan is the Robert Quartermain assistant professor of gender and sexuality in the Faculty of Education at the University of British Columbia. Harper's work broadly addresses how adults teach young children to make sense of the social world.

Keon M. McGuire (he/him/his) is an associate professor of higher and postsecondary education in the Mary Lou Fulton Teachers College and a faculty affiliate with the School of Social Transformation. McGuire's research agenda focuses on the status and experiences of minoritized students across postsecondary educational settings. Drawing from Africana frameworks, McGuire examines how race, gender, and religion shape minoritized college students' everyday experiences. Additionally, McGuire investigates the ways racism, sexism, and heteronormativity undermine the experiences of minoritized college students as well as they ways students resist and respond to such marginalization. In 2019, he was named a National Academy of Education (NAEd)/Spencer postdoctoral fellow and ACPA Emerging Scholar.

Steve D. Mobley Jr. is an assistant professor of higher education administration at The University of Alabama. His scholarship focuses on the contemporary placement of historically Black colleges and universities (HBCUs). Particularly, his research underscores and highlights the understudied facets of HBCU communities, including issues surrounding race, social class, and student sexuality.

Angie Morrill (Klamath Tribes) is the program director for Title VI Indian Education for Portland Public Schools.

Sam Museus is professor of education studies at the University of California, San Diego (UCSD) and founding director of the National Institute for Transformation and Equity (NITE). His research agenda is focused on diversity and equity, social movements and activism, and transforming systems to be more inclusive and equitable.

Chris A. Nelson (K'awaika and Diné) is assistant professor at the University of Denver's Higher Education Department. She utilizes a blending of critical theory and Indigenous relationality theory to explore the purpose and function of higher education.

Z Nicolazzo is an associate professor of trans* studies in education at The University of Arizona.

Leigh Patel is a writer, educator, and cultural worker. Her work is based in the knowledge that as long as oppression has existed so have freedom struggles. She is a community-based researcher as well as an eldercare provider. Prior to being employed as a professor, she was a middle school language arts teacher, a journalist, and a state-level policymaker. She is also a proud national board member of Education for Liberation, a nonprofit that focuses on supporting low-income people, particularly youth of color, to understand and challenge the injustices their communities face.

Patel's writing ranges from short essays for public outlets, such as Beacon Broadside, NPR, The Conversation and The Feminist Wire, and *The Chronicle for Higher Education.* Her latest book, *There Is No Study Without Struggle: Confronting Settler Colonialism in Higher Education* (2021), from Beacon Press connects the distinct yet deeply connected forms of oppression while also shedding light on the crucial nature of political education for social transformation. Her walk-on song is "Can I Kick It" by ATCQ. You can follow her on twitter @lipatel.

Leilani Sabzalian (Alutiiq) is an assistant professor of Indigenous studies in education at the University of Oregon and codirector of the Sapsik'ʷałá (Teacher) Education program.

Heather J. Shotton (Wichita/Kiowa/Cheyenne) is a citizen of the Wichita and Affiliated Tribes. She is an associate professor and chair of educational leadership and policy studies at the University of Oklahoma on the traditional homelands of the Hasinai (Caddo) and Kitikiti'sh (Wichita) peoples.

She also serves as the director of Indigenous education initiatives for the Jeannine Rainbolt College of Education.

Amanda R. Tachine is Navajo from Ganado, Arizona. She is Náneesht'éžhí Táchii'nii (Zuni Red Running into Water clan) born for Tł'ízí'łání (Many Goats clan). She is an assistant professor in educational leadership and innovation at Arizona State University.

Leonard D. Taylor, Jr. is an assistant professor of higher education administration at Auburn University. He holds a PhD in organizational leadership, policy, and development from the University of Minnesota Twin Cities. Through research he interrogates and seeks to advance how administrators, faculty, and staff members support student success in higher education contexts.

Amy C. Wang is a PhD student in the Education Studies department at UCSD.

K. Wayne Yang writes about decolonization and everyday epic organizing, particularly from underneath ghetto colonialism, often with his frequent collaborator Eve Tuck, and sometimes for an avatar called la paperson. Currently, they are convening The Land Relationships Super Collective with several Indigenous and non-Indigenous community organizations engaged in land-based projects. Yang's work transgresses the line between scholarship and community, as evidenced by his involvement in urban education and community organizing. Before his academic career, he was a public school-teacher in Lisjan Ohlone territory, now called Oakland, California, where he cofounded the Avenues Project, a youth development nonprofit organization, as well as East Oakland Community High School, which were inspired by the survival programs of the Black Panther Party. He is provost of Muir College and professor in ethnic studies at UCSD.

Irene H. Yoon is associate professor of educational leadership and policy at The University of Utah. Grounded by a love agenda, her research is concerned with leadership and teaching in public schools that contribute to equity, justice, and empowering learning environments for teachers and youth.

INDEX

For Product Safety Concerns and Information please contact our EU
representative GPSR@taylorandfrancis.com
Taylor & Francis Verlag GmbH, Kaufingerstraße 24, 80331 München, Germany

www.ingramcontent.com/pod-product-compliance
Lightning Source LLC
Chambersburg PA
CBHW050655280326
41932CB00015B/2913